CW01347515

LANDS

SO FAR

THE ONGOING STORY OF A FAMILY BUSINESS
OVER 150 YEARS
BY
TOM LAND

First Published 1997

Published by Land Instruments International Ltd., Dronfield S18 1DJ, Derbyshire. England.

© Land Instruments International Ltd., 1997. All rights reserved. No part of this book may be reproduced or utilised in any form, electronic or mechanical, including photocopying or recording, or by storage or retrieval system, without permission from the publishers.

ISBN 0 9530726 0 6

Printed in England by Ladas Printers Ltd.,
Speedwell Industrial Estate, Staveley, Chesterfield S43 3PF.

CONTENTS

INTRODUCTION

Lands in silver plate and cutlery	2
The way the new business grew	2
The growth of people and of funds	4
Building a fine business that is a good place to work	4
This is the story as I saw it	5
Lands so far	5
The many people who have contributed to the story and its telling	6

CHAPTER 1

A HUNDRED YEARS IN THE ELECTROPLATE TRADE   7

Cutlery and silver in Sheffield	7
Henry Land	8
The electroplating of silver and gold	9
Harriss and Land	10
Henry Land & Co.	10
Tom Land, my grandfather	11
Trouble with his brothers	13
Partnership with Walter Oxley	13
Frank Land	14
Trouble with the Union	15
In 1906 the firm becomes T. Land & Son Ltd	16
Benefits and restraints in a non-union company	17
The 'model' factory that they built at Queens Road	17
Frank's invention of 'machine engraving'	18
The first World War	21
Frank fights for the survival of the business	21
We are shut out of the Australian market	22
Survival by Boots and pewter	22
Concentrate and Simplify	25
Don't go into the plate trade, Tom	26
Cambridge - and learning a trade	26
Learning from Father	27
Another war	28

CHAPTER 2

MY SEVEN YEARS AT JESSOPS   31
Wm. Jessop & Sons Ltd.   31
My job at Jessops   31
Measuring the temperature of liquid steel   32
Developing a special recorder for the job   34
Exploring the temperature variations in a furnace   35
Making a few thermocouples at Queens Road   36
Designing a better radiation pyrometer for the open hearth furnace   36
Measuring hot surfaces below red heat - in cold surroundings   37
I patent the idea of a pyrometer with a hemispherical mirror attached   38
Donald Oliver starts up the BSA Group Research Centre, which I join   39
I go to Power Jets and learn to design a small jet engine   40

CHAPTER 3

THE FOUNDING OF LAND PYROMETERS   41
I have to decide my future career   41
I set out to build an industrial instrument company - cautiously   41
We engage Roy Marsh   42
A business like the Amalgams Company   43
The new business grows fast   44
My cousin Eric Land joins the family business   45
We split off Land Pyrometers   46
Learning to be engineers - and accountants   46
Designing equipment that is high class and 'user-friendly'   48
Finance for the growing business   49
The electroplate and pewter business is sold   50
Where do we go from here?   50
We get financial investment from ICFC   52
A dramatic change of policy   53
Doing the unthinkable   54
Celebration   55
Building a factory at Dronfield   57

CHAPTER 4

THE ELECTRONITE CONNECTION   59
Disposable liquid steel thermocouples   59
A visit from Henk Kleyn   60

The patent litigation in America	61
We sell more shares to ICFC to meet family death duties	61
We start to manufacture Dipstiks	61
Dipstiks soon double our thermocouple sales	62
Bill Longley and Tony Duncan become directors of Land Pyrometers	62
The Sampla and the Leigh oxygen probe	64
Land Europe, a failure	65
The profitable seventies	65
Adjusting for inflation	66
U.K. steel production crashes in 1980 but we get by	66

CHAPTER 5

RADIATION PYROMETERS AT QUEENS ROAD

RADIATION PYROMETERS AT QUEENS ROAD	69
The Land Surface Pyrometer	69
A radiation pyrometer for Kents	72
A stable zero	73
Getting rid of glare	73
The spherical calibrating furnace	74
Learning to manufacture instruments	75
The range of pyrometers expands	76
The international dimension	77
Getting started in America	78
I meet Fred Maltby	78
Don Nielsen begins to sell Land products	80
Travelling the great American highways	80
The silicon "solar" cell - wow!	82
The turbine blade pyrometer	83

CHAPTER 6

BIGGER SIGNALS, BIGGER SALES

BIGGER SIGNALS, BIGGER SALES	85
The move to Dronfield	85
Capturing the fleeting signal	86
Bigger signals	86
The "parrot's perch" experiment	87
Putting an amplifier in the thermometer head	88
ElectroNite become our distributors	88
We win the Armco competition	88
ElectroNite widen their horizons	90
ElectroNite in trouble	91

We decide to form our own company in U.S.A.	91
Eric Land is appointed Managing Director but I remain an active chairman	91
The development of System 2	92
The Infrared Division gets its own Sales Department 1973	93
Roy Barber takes control of Infrared Sales	94

CHAPTER 7

THE NEXT GENERATION - JASMINE JOINS THE BUSINESS 95

The burner control project	95
Jasmine joins the team working on Burner Control	96
Jasmine's arrival causes a family crisis; we form Land Combustion	98
Dave Coe leaves Land Combustion and Jasmine becomes Managing Director	99
Hard times at Land Pyrometers in the early eighties.	100
I devise a plan to buy out my cousin Eric Land and reorganize the business	100
We form Land Instruments International Ltd and Eric resigns	102
The management structure of Land Instruments International Ltd	103
We buy the factory next door	105
Jasmine becomes Managing Director of Land Instruments International	106

CHAPTER 8

LAND PYROMETERS HAS TO BE SOLD 109

Tony takes over Land Pyrometers in dangerous times	110
Fred Campbell dies; Tony takes control of all functions at Land Pyrometers	110
We begin to sell the ElectroNite 'Celox' oxygen probe	111
Henk Kleyn organizes a management buy-out of ElectroNite	112
ElectroNite is sold to Heraeus and we have to sell Land Pyrometers to them	113

CHAPTER 9

LAND INFRARED UNDER ROY BARBER 115

The Rolls Royce saga	115
Other Turbine Applications	117
The Great American market	118
Portables	123
Thermal imagers	124
Marketing	126
Microprocessors and System 3	128
Organization and staff	130
Russia and Svet	131

Visiting China	132
Roy's Summary	134
Visiting the foreign Customer	134

CHAPTER 10

THE TURBULENT HISTORY OF LAND COMBUSTION	137
How we got into combustion instrumentation	137
The theory of suction pyrometers	138
The combustion of coal and other fuels	138
We begin to manufacture probes for measurements in power station boilers	139
Burner control	140
The work at Winnington	140
The acid dew-point meter	141
I work out the theory of the acid dew-point meter	142
Measuring carbon monoxide in the waste gases	143
The cross-correlation flame monitor	143
Land Combustion at Sheepbridge	145
Land Combustion Inc.	145
Successes and failures	146
Dave Coe leaves to start his own business	147
Jasmine becomes Managing Director of Land Combustion	148
Ramon Biarnes takes charge of the American subsidiary.	148
Ramon starts to run the Combustion business from Philadelphia	149

CHAPTER 11

LANDS RENEWED	151
Jasmine takes my place as head of a new management team	151
LAND COMBUSTION IN THE NINETIES	152
How Land Combustion languished during the early eighties	152
THINK AMERICA!	153
Dust and Opacity monitoring	155
Combustion Efficiency	156
Flue Gas Analysers	157
Portable Gas Analysers	158
Other Products	159
Production	159
LAND INFRARED IN THE NINETIES	160
An accountant in charge of Land Infrared	160
Production	162

System 4	162
Scanners	163
Thermal imaging	165
Fibre optics	165
Svet's idea in action	165
Product philosophy	166
Centralisation v. Localisation	166
New building at Dronfield	167

CHAPTER 12

QUALITY AND STANDARDS 169
A tradition of quality and accuracy 169
Land Infrared 170
Land Combustion 174

CHAPTER 13

SOME THINGS THAT I HAVE LEARNT 175
What we have achieved together in 50 years 175
A working community that makes money and serves its customers well 176
Concentration and world-wide sales 176
Good people at the heart of the business 177
The organization 178
Removing the barriers to enthusiasm 179
Learning the skills 180
Financial control 181
A good place to work 181
The future 182

Henry Land and his Family

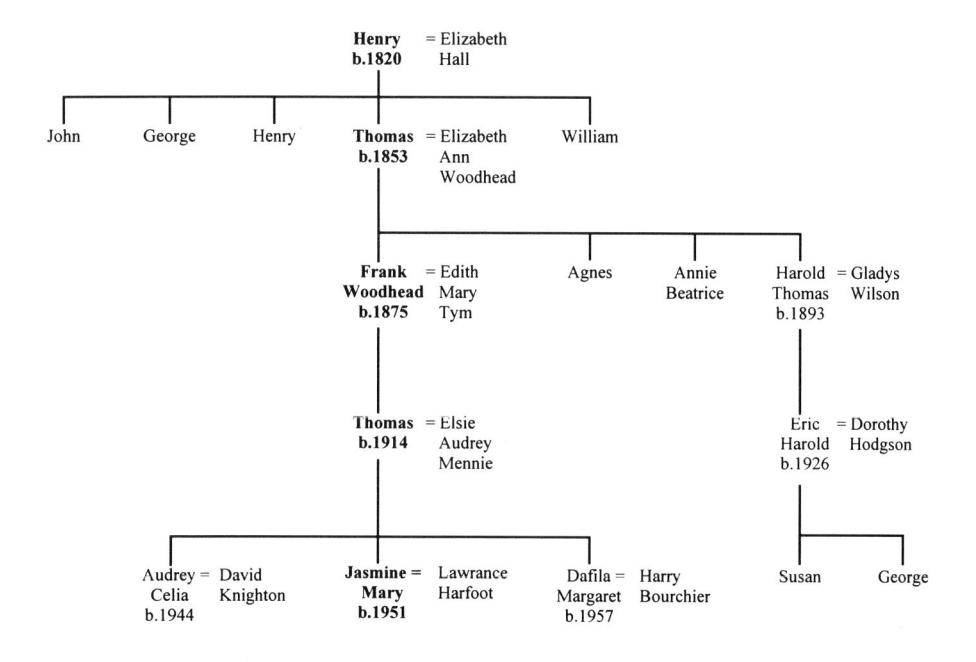

- **Henry b.1820** = Elizabeth Hall
  - John
  - George
  - Henry
  - **Thomas b.1853** = Elizabeth Ann Woodhead
    - **Frank Woodhead b.1875** = Edith Mary Tym
      - **Thomas b.1914** = Elsie Audrey Mennie
        - Audrey Celia b.1944 = David Knighton
        - **Jasmine Mary b.1951** = Lawrance Harfoot
        - Dafila Margaret b.1957 = Harry Bourchier
    - Agnes
    - Annie Beatrice
    - Harold Thomas b.1893 = Gladys Wilson
      - Eric Harold b.1926 = Dorothy Hodgson
        - Susan
        - George
  - William

Land Instruments International - Long Service Personnel

LAND instruments international
LONG SERVICE PERSONNEL

OVER 35 YEARS
- Tom Land
- Roy Barber

OVER 30 YEARS
- John Bamford
- John Davenport
- Jim Lycett
- Peter Fearnehough
- Michael Tilly
- Martin Johnston

OVER 25 YEARS
- David Bellamy
- John Ellis
- Max Yates
- Michael Ward
- Alan Moore
- Jeanette White
- Tony Duncan
- Norman Loasby
- David Hebblethwaite
- Michael Brown

OVER 20 YEARS
- Marjorie Whitehead
- Maureen Limb
- Jeanette Simpson
- Virginia Harris
- Gillian Pearson
- Peter Kirby
- Michael Harries
- Michael Gilday
- Pat Wing
- Peter Nuttall
- Richard Williams
- David Chapman
- Pauline Speechley
- Ian Goldsbrough
- Tim Childs
- Ian Powell
- Sandra Giles
- Nigel Wormald
- David Massey

OVER 15 YEARS
- Ian Thorley
- Dennis Smith
- Ken Greaves
- Annette Sneesby
- Deborah Jacklin
- Gary Wolstenholme
- Frank Shepherd
- Ronald Mather

- Geoff Beynon
- Pamela Morton
- David Leadley
- Mark Connor
- Neil Oxley
- Norman Fisher
- Graham Shaw
- Robert Staniforth
- Paul Lee
- May Heslop
- Jasmine Harfoot
- Douglas Easthope
- Robert Allen
- Tom McDougall
- Peter Fern
- Gillian Helliwell
- Ian Ridley
- Andrew Mellor
- Wanda Lang
- Lynda Ball
- Rita Smith
- Gerald Amos
- Pam Fearnehough
- Ramon Biornes
- Richard Gagg
- David Footitt
- Jim Tattersall
- John Marples
- Julie Hunt

- Ralph Payne
- Gail Peat
- Sue Slater
- Malcolm Gillott

OVER 10 YEARS
- Ian Bagshaw
- Val Gilday
- Audrey Williamson
- Helen Singleton
- Stuart Metcalfe
- Paul Coates
- John Dixon
- John Greatorex
- David Amory
- John Hern
- Mike Lutz
- Janet Norton
- Lesley Hallam
- Richard Moore
- John Hyde
- Rosemary Hayes
- Susan Hutton
- Mark North
- Steve Swain
- Nicole Bagshaw
- Dennis Dixon
- Tim Swift
- Peter Mackey
- Lyndon Jones

- Jim Hobson
- Andrew Tattershall
- Sue Fairbrother
- Roy Footitt
- Michael O'Connell
- Dave Atkinson
- Robert Elfstrom
- Winifred Clark
- Ed Sanderson
- Michelle Wade
- Jean Wheatman
- Michel Devos
- Luanne Dipaola
- Rich Parella

INTRODUCTION

I have written this book for the people who work for Lands all over the world and for those who in the future will come to work with us. I have written it to celebrate 50 years of Lands as an instrument company. But the family has been in business in Sheffield for much longer than that and I think that you will be interested to go right back to the beginning and read how it all began in about 1845 when my great-grand father Henry Land started a little business of his own.

Fig. A Tom Land, the Author.

For a hundred years Lands was one among many Sheffield manufacturers of tableware and cutlery. Fifty years ago, at the end of the Second World War, that long-established industry had dwindled to such a pitiful condition that we knew that there was no profitable future in it for us. If we were to continue and prosper we would need to make the perilous transition to a different industry. By that time I was 32 years old and my father was in his early seventies so it was my job to find a new field of work for the family. I chose to go into something that I understood and I chose industrial instrumentation.

Lands in silver plate and cutlery

The first chapter of the book tells the story of those first hundred years in the electroplate trade, which also included a certain amount of cutlery manufacture. The family never made a great fortune and no member of the family was ever Master Cutler or Lord Mayor of Sheffield, but my father and my grandfather built up a business which at one time employed more than a hundred people. They worked hard in times that were rarely easy but they knew how to run a business and they had good cause to be proud of what they achieved.

When my father was in his early eighties I asked him to tell me all that he remembered about the old days and I wrote it down on both sides of two large sheets of note paper. Fortunately I kept it safely and when I went to the public library to check the facts and figures from old copies of the Sheffield Directory everything that I could find confirmed his story. Other books in the Local History section filled in the background of Sheffield in the 19th century. One written by an American named Jack. L. Scott and called "Pewter Wares from Sheffield" (Antiquary Press, Baltimore) includes details about the Land business. I hope that you will find the chapter interesting in itself; I intended it to serve as a prologue to the main story, which is the development of Land Instruments International but you may find it the best part!

I joined the family business in 1935 after taking a degree in mathematics and physics at Cambridge University, and worked in the pewter and electroplate business until 1939. During the war I worked as a physicist in charge of temperature measurement (pyrometry) at the steel works of Wm. Jessop and Sons Ltd. Those six years changed the direction of my life.

The work that I did at Jessops allowed me to start a new business in pyrometry, which first supplemented and then replaced the old electroplate business. So the old T. Land & Son Ltd. died and from its ashes rose Land Pyrometers Ltd., which in turn became Land Instruments International Ltd.

My father had been in a declining industry, capturing a larger and larger share of a shrinking market. Now we were in a growing market. As the instrumental control of manufacturing processes became more and more important, we were able to ride on the crest of a wave. Plenty of companies in the instrument industry fell off their surfboards but the wave was rolling if you could ride it and we were able to keep our business growing year after year.

The way the new business grew

It turned out that we built not one new business but three. If you look at the following chart you will see how the three businesses developed over the years. I have plotted the sales generated by the three businesses on the curves marked 'ALL' and 'infrared and combustion'. There is a heading across the top that explains that the graphs on the chart are in pounds of 1995 value. A pound of today's money is worth only one tenth as much as a pound was worth in 1950 so I have recorded all the annual sales values in pounds of the same low value that we are accustomed to today. This allows us to see the true extent of our growth, undistorted by inflation.

Across the bottom of the chart you will see the dates running from 1945 to 2000 and up the left-hand side you will see the values of our sales year by year in millions of pounds. For the first ten years we sold very little but thermocouples and spares. This part of the business was a good, profitable little business. It was always called Land Pyrometers until it had to be sold in 1989. I have written its history in Chapters 3 and 4 and its last few years in Chapter 8.

The instrument business that we now call Land Infrared grew up as part of Land Pyrometers but it was always a very different kind of business. I have chosen to tell its story separately in Chapters 5 and 6 and then in Chapter 8. It was not making any significant contribution until about 1960 but it grew and grew until in 1981 its sales exceeded those of Land Pyrometers. Land Combustion followed a decade or more later. Notice that the graph is plotted on a logarithmic scale.

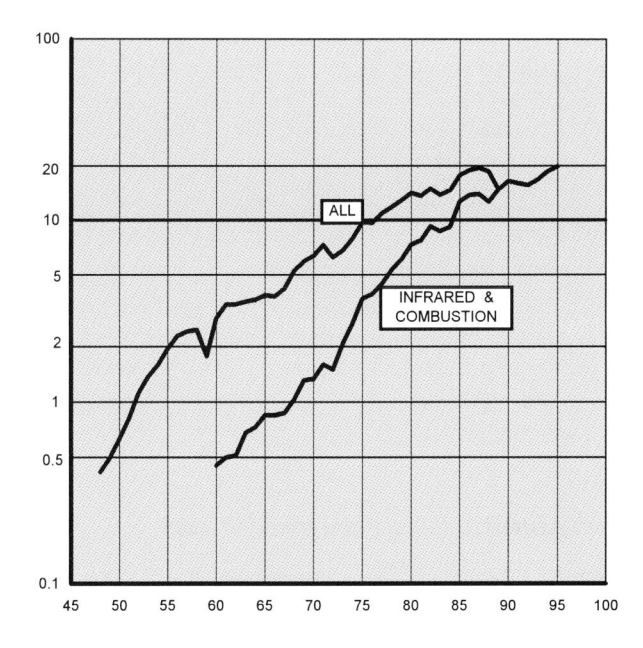

Fig. B The growth of the business.

The three businesses were run as a single unit until 1980 when Land Combustion was formed as a separate company. Jasmine had joined the new Combustion Division in 1977 and Chapter 7 tells how she steadily gained experience and responsibility until I was able to hand over the business to her in 1987. Her arrival had caused a family crisis. In 1983 I bought out my cousin Eric Land and we reorganized the business to form Land Instruments International Ltd. which brought its three component parts together again. This time the three divisions were separately managed, an arrangement that has worked very well.

The steady growth of the post-war business makes it look like one long success story, but living through it was not like that at all. There were times when the business went all wrong and times when we failed to grow for several years on end. Several times we found ourselves in serious trouble and we had to dig ourselves out; the graph shows merely a dip or a flat and off we go again. Our continuous growth over a period of 50 years is something that we can be proud of.

The growth of people and of funds

It was not only the sales that grew. We had no magic source of funds with which to finance our growth. We had to plough back our profits year after year and make sure that the profits gave us sufficient funds to finance the growth. With these retained profits we built a new factory and extended it; we bought machines and equipment, cars and vans, and renewed them over and again. We financed ever greater stocks of materials and work in progress and (something that you might forget) the goods that our customers had bought but not yet paid for. Our funds marched in step with our growing sales once we had learnt how to make good profits.

The third and most important thing that grew was people. Starting with just three people in 1947, the numbers grew to 300 by 1989 when we sold Land Pyrometers; it now stands at about 280. But numbers are not the most important thing. A business prospers because of the quality and enthusiasm of the people that work in it. At Jessops I had found that it was not impossible to be the best in my chosen corner. I always insisted that we should aim to be much better than our competitors. When you are known to be the best it is much easier to recruit the best people and give everyone pride in working for a good company.

Building a fine business that is a good place to work

I was always ambitious to build a fine business, not just a bigger business. A fine business is a business that serves its customers well, that grows and prospers and makes sufficient profit to finance its growth. It is also a good place to work. We spend a large part of our lives at work and a good manager will aim to make his business a place where people can enjoy working, can feel at home and know that they will be dealt with honestly and with respect and consideration. I always distrusted the almost universal convention that used to divide the employees of most companies into "staff" and "workpeople", granted very different treatment and privileges for no valid reason. I was aware that if I were treated as a second-class citizen I would be tempted to deliver in return second-class service to the Company. We were one of the earliest companies to appreciate the foolishness of this policy. We therefore set out to build a business in which there would be no second class citizens. The chief opposition to such a plan came from those whose privileged status was threatened. Slowly, over the years, we chipped away at the old order until we finally have homogeneous working conditions. Everyone works a 35 hour week, and is paid a monthly salary by bank transfer, everyone in the U.K. is in the same pension scheme, and everyone receives a share of the profits generated by the business. We have become a working community.

This is the story as I saw it

This account that I have written is a personal one and when I read it through it seems to be all too full of Me. I could only show you the growth of the business through my own eyes. I am keenly aware that one person's account could never be totally objective - history is like that - and another person would view many incidents quite differently. I have tried to be as honest and unprejudiced as I can and I hope that the reader will find it interesting. I am aware that this account may easily find its way into the hands of others in the same line of business - and why not? With that thought in mind I have decided that history might wisely be defined for the purposes of this book as coming to an end in 1995.

As the business has grown it has increasingly become based on applied science, which is a reflection of the fact that my personal abilities have lain in applied physics. It is wise to concentrate on doing the things that you are good at. It would be foolish to gloss over the basic science that lies at the roots of our company. I have done my best to explain any technical details simply and clearly. In case anyone should find the technical bits hard to follow I have introduced cross-headings so that you can skip a few paragraphs without losing track of the story.

Lands so far

I have called this book 'Lands so far' for two reasons. First it means that Lands has already come a long way; second it means that I am telling a story that is far from finished. When I look back and see how completely different Lands is from ten or fifteen years ago I realize that I am writing only a progress report on a story that has yet to reveal the most amazing sequel to this early beginning. Those of you who are working at Lands are starting to write that sequel now.

The many people who have contributed to the story and its telling

Our business has been successful not primarily for reason of its family ownership but rather because so many competent people have contributed so much to it. In telling the story I have mentioned the names of some people who made interesting and important contributions. Stories have to be told that way. But no show is a success on the stage without a competent and enthusiastic supporting cast. Before I go any farther I want to thank all the many people who have helped to make Lands a successful business and a good place to work. Without you all there would have been no story to tell.

I must also record my thanks to the many people who have helped me in writing this book. My wife has cheerfully put up with the disruption of a properly ordered retirement and has made many helpful suggestions, as have Jasmine and her husband Larry and other members of my family. David Knighton, Celia's husband, used his experience as a university lecturer to make many suggestions for improving the text.

Above all I am grateful to Roy Barber who wrote for me an account of the period after 1974 during which I had little direct contact with Land Infrared. I have quoted freely from his notes in Chapter 9. He also made useful suggestions about this book and, of course, contributed enormously, over a period now approaching 50 years, to the development and the management of the business. Finally I would like to thank Tom McDougall and his team from the P & P Dept. of Land Infrared, particularly Michelle Wade, who took my written document and the illustrations and turned them into a book.

CHAPTER 1
A HUNDRED YEARS IN THE ELECTROPLATE TRADE
1843 to 1939

Cutlery and silver in Sheffield

I find that family histories can be quite fascinating and I hope that you will enjoy this story of my family and its varied fortunes. If you should get bored with our early history you can skip to the last page of this chapter and begin again with Chapter 2 where you will find the origins of the instrument business that now has the grand title of Land Instruments International Limited.

For more than a hundred years the Land family business was a typical small-to-middling Sheffield family business, based on the manufacture of pewter and EPBM teasets, tankards, prize cups and all kinds of domestic tableware to meet the needs and whims of the day. I had better begin by explaining what "pewter" and "EPBM" mean and what place these wares took in the range of products made in Sheffield at that time. Sheffield has been famous for its cutlery since the Middle Ages. It has also been one of the few towns with an assay office where silver and gold can be marked. All kinds of tableware were made in silver: teapots and coffee pots, jugs and trays, forks and spoons.

In 1743 Thomas Boulsover had invented a method of fusing together an ingot of copper and two much thinner ingots of silver and of rolling the composite ingot into a sheet of copper 'plated' on both sides with a thin layer of silver. This composite sheet was used in place of sterling silver to make a wide range of beautiful tableware which came to be known as Sheffield plate.

Sheffield plate was less expensive than silver but it was not cheap. The metal used in most tableware was pewter, which is a tin-based alloy that is easily worked, easy to spin on a lathe or shape under a drop-stamp, easy to cast in moulds and to solder. The best pewter contains about 90% tin with antimony and copper added to harden it. In the eighteenth century pewter was commonly known as French metal; but in the latter part of the century the French were not universally popular in England so a more patriotic name was needed. Some bright fellow began to call it Britannia metal and the name caught on. So we find tableware marked either PEWTER or BM. When electroplating arrived the mark was changed to EPBM, meaning electro-plated Britannia metal. In the early nineteenth century Sheffield was the principal centre of manufacture of Britannia metal.

Henry Land

The Land family came to Sheffield from Wakefield. In 1815 my great-great-grandfather Francis Land was wounded at the Battle of Waterloo. My grandfather told me that when he sat on his grandfather's knee as a little boy he was allowed to feel the bullet that was still lodged in his grandfather's side.

Francis' son Henry came to Sheffield, perhaps with his parents, where he was apprenticed to the trade of horn pressing - horn was used in the manufacture of cutlery. He left to become a commercial traveller in a firm that manufactured Britannia metal ware. He needed a steady job as he married before he completed his apprenticeship. Nevertheless he soon decided to go into business himself. His father had once had a mill in Wakefield but Henry became a manufacturer of Britannia metal tableware.

Fig. 1.1 Henry Land and his wife Eliza.

In the early nineteenth century Sheffield was the home of the 'little mesters', who each employed a few craftsmen. They made cutlery and edge tools (knives, saws, chisels, scythes etc.) for home, farm and factory as well as tableware and fine silver. They were independent, skilled individuals, accustomed to making their way in the world and to taking the rough with the smooth. Most of them worked within five or ten minutes walk of each other, and lived within the same small area in the centre of the town. If you decided to set up as a manufacturer you could have much of the work done by such people as out-workers.

My father told me how, as a boy, he would be given an ingot of metal to carry on his shoulder to the rolling mill and bring it back the same way. So a young man like Henry Land could start a manufacturing business without investing too much capital. Perhaps there was a bit of money in the family to give him a start.

The electroplating of silver and gold

In business you need to be intelligent and hard working if you are to succeed. You also need to be a bit lucky and to grasp your chance with both hands when it turns up. Henry Land was lucky enough to start his business just when a great opportunity for bright young men turned up in exactly the trade that he had chosen. In Birmingham the Elkington cousins had learnt of the invention by a medical man called Dr. Wright of the cyanide process for plating silver and gold. They took this remarkable invention and brought it to the point at which it was a practicable industrial process, which they patented. The Elkingtons decided that the best way to exploit their invention would be to license it to manufacturers of tableware. After receiving a cool reception from most of the firms that they approached, they eventually found more success with the manufacturers of Britannia metal ware in Sheffield.

I suspect that the electroplating of gold and silver may have been the first major application of electricity to an industrial process. No wonder it was viewed with so much scepticism when it was first demonstrated. The railway had only arrived in Sheffield in 1838 and that was enough of a novelty for most people. It was only in 1800 that Count Alessandro Volta had invented the first electric battery and had demonstrated that it produced a continuous current of electricity. As a source of electric current Henry still had to rely on primary cells of the same general family as those that we use as torch batteries; his batteries were not convenient little dry batteries, but big jars containing chemical solutions and electrodes that had to be taken out every morning and scrubbed with a wire brush under running water.

Forty years later, when Henry taught my father (his grandson) about electroplating, he used the same type of battery to provide the electric current that he passed through the solution of silver in potassium cyanide in his plating vats. The current passed from sheets of pure silver suspended in the liquid on both sides of the vat to the spoons or teapots hanging in the middle, carrying the silver and depositing it on the tableware being plated. Fig. 1.2 shows one of our platers (Beattie) putting a teapot into the plating vat at Queens Road. Of course the cyanide is a very powerful poison; my father used to tell me that we had enough poison in our vats to poison the whole of Sheffield, which was probably true. We consider ourselves a high-technology company today, but in his day Henry Land was equally advanced in his technology.

Fig. 1.2 Putting a teapot in a silver plating vat.

Harriss and Land

My father told me that Henry Land was one of the three first 'students' to go to Birmingham to learn how to carry out this extraordinary process. At Surrey Street Methodist chapel Henry had met George Harriss who manufactured spoons and forks, and they had gone into partnership as Harriss & Land, manufacturers of Britannia metal and spoons and forks. When Henry went to Elkingtons my father said that he went with Mr. Brook of Brook Brothers and George Walker who founded Walker & Hall, one of the biggest names in the business. Jack Scott, in his book, states that George Walker was an unemployed knife grinder when he was taken on by John Harrison and sent to Elkingtons to learn electroplating.

Henry Land & Co.

The partnership of Henry Land and George Harriss must have been a successful one for it lasted nearly 20 years. Jack Scott writes in his book that in 1864 Henry Land advertised his company as "late Land and Harriss". My grandfather was not quite sure of the date on which the partnership ended and took a reasonable guess when he printed on his note paper "established 1860". Grandfather was only a little boy when it happened. The partnership had operated from 57 Arundel Street and later moved to number 83. When my grandfather was born the family lived in the next street to their factory at 96 Arundel Lane. I have a copy of his birth certificate registered by his mother Eliza Land née Hall who signed her name with a cross. The site of his birthplace is now occupied by Sheffield Hallam University.

My father told me that Henry prospered quickly when he had the business for himself again. He lived in a large house on fashionable Glossop Road and drove to work in a carriage and pair. My grandfather had large oil paintings of Henry and his wife that had an air of substantial prosperity. Sadly, after the death of his wife Henry started drinking and neglected his business. He finally disposed of his business 'in a fit of drunkenness' some time after 1870. He died in Leeds in about 1895 and is buried in the Sheffield general cemetery, Cemetery Road. The American Civil War seriously affected Sheffield business and may have contributed to Henry's problems but his sons were probably a bigger factor.

Henry had five sons who all went into the business. My father said that his uncles were a wild lot, brought up in luxury, amusing and talented, good company and partial to a pint. With the loss of the business their easy life was over and they had to fend for themselves. Uncle George became a silver finisher; Father said he never saw him drunk but he never saw him sober. One uncle became a circus performer - I think a trapeze artist, something athletic. Another turned up at Grandfather's house in the middle of the night, broke; he had walked all the way from Glasgow.

Tom Land, my grandfather

The fourth son, Tom, was a different type. He had attended Wolstenholm's College until he was 17. In my father's words, Tom 'was intended for the administration of the factory', but sadly the business collapsed and he had to start again from nothing. He was my grandfather. His photograph (Fig. 1.3) shows him as I remember him, as an old man.

Fig. 1.3 My grandfather, also Tom Land.

When he was young he was tall with black curly hair and a fine black moustache. My father said that when you walked behind him you could see the ends of his moustache from behind!

My grandfather had a cheerful and optimistic disposition and was always ready to 'have a go.' At the age of 19, with no money and no workplace he set about building himself a business. My father told me once that grandfather was a man that everybody trusted. He must have seemed a young man worth helping because a friend who made brass taps offered him a room over his factory and stood surety for him at the bank as he was a minor.

In this upstairs room young Tom used his skill as a craftsman to spin small articles (salt-cellars, mustard-pots etc.) which he made up and sold to the trade. His little business prospered. Somehow some plating vats and their precious solutions had been saved from the wreck of Henry Land & Co.. Tom installed them in his workshop so that he could silver plate and gild the articles he made and could sell finished goods. My grandfather once told me that he had said that he would marry the prettiest girl in Sheffield and that he did. The pretty girl that he married in 1874 was Elizabeth Ann Woodhead. They lived at 13 Cheney Row, which was demolished a hundred years ago to build the present town hall. My father was born there; he told me that his bedroom window looked over the graveyard of St. Paul's church and he was frightened to think of all those dead people buried there. The church was destroyed in the Sheffield blitz and the graveyard is now the Peace Gardens. Before she would marry him Annie insisted that Tom should 'sign the pledge', which he did. The devastating effect of drink on Henry Land was a bitter lesson that our family never forgot. My father often told me how his grandfather would be brought home filthy after being found lying in the gutter.

Fig. 1.4 Tom Dale spinning a teapot body.

He was also amazed that next morning his grandfather would be up and out again in top hat and frock coat with his silver topped cane as if nothing had happened.

Trouble with his brothers

Tom had trouble with his brothers who began to treat this new business as a bit of a family affair from which they were entitled to a few pickings. So when they were short of money they would take finished goods from the factory to sell. My father told me that in the end his father took the drastic step of putting his business in his wife's name; when I went to the library I found in the Sheffield Directory and in Jack Scott's book the entry: 'Elizabeth Ann Land, E.P. and Gilder.' Perhaps they were more afraid of Annie than of Tom; anyway I understand that the stratagem was successful and there was no more trouble.

Having sorted out the problems with his father and his brothers, my grandfather was able to start the long job of rebuilding the business that his father had squandered and which he had expected to manage. The more I have thought about his life and his achievements the more similarities I have seen between his life and mine. Of course I had a vastly better family position to start from, but the need to make a fresh start was the same, and the same problems of financing a growing business had to be solved. Even the rate at which his business grew was much the same as mine. Within 30 years he was employing about 120 people, which is much the same as we did at Land Pyrometers. But I was much more fortunate in having a nice factory of our own at Queens Road. My grandfather rented his factory space and kept moving every few years to one a bit bigger a few hundred yards away as he needed more space.

Partnership with Walter Oxley

In Victorian times it was not so easy to arrange a loan from the Bank or from a friendly financial institution. It was more usual to find some wealthier acquaintance to help with extra capital. Tom was able to obtain a loan from a Mr. Tandy, who was a comb manufacturer, when he moved to larger premises in Hermitage Lane in 1887. Unfortunately this arrangement did not work well. In 1890 Walter Oxley, who was a friend at Cherry Tree Methodist Church in Nether Edge, offered to lend Tom the money to pay off Mr. Tandy and they went into partnership as Land and Oxley at Beta Works, Fitzwilliam Street. Walter Oxley was a cutler and brought with him his knowledge of the cutlery trade. The Sheffield Directory of 1895-6 records 'Land & Oxley, Nimrod Works, 111 Eldon St., Manufacturers of EPBM, spoons and forks and table knives.'

The partnership with Walter Oxley was "very successful", my father records, "both in friendship and commerce". The growth of the business demanded further extension so the firm moved in about 1897 to Nelson Works, 107 Trafalgar Street. That was a fine, patriotic address to put on your letter heading!

Fig. 1.5 Frank Land, my father.

Frank Land

Tom had a son, Frank and two daughters, Agnes and Beatrice. Much later a little surprise arrived in the shape of a second son, Harold who was 18 years younger than Frank. Frank was a bright boy, usually top of his class at Saint Matthias School. When he was 12 the headmaster of his school came to see his father to plead for him to be left at school to continue his education. Tom was adamant; he needed Frank in the business and Frank must leave school - and he did. Frank, who was my father, never quite forgave his father for cutting his education short. He read widely and studied design, in which he was very talented, at the Sheffield School of Art. He became a well-educated man and his practical knowledge of every aspect of the business enabled him to take charge of the business before he was 40.

Frank had learnt metal-smithing on Saturday mornings from the age of 9. He learnt to solder, as was then done, with a candle and a blow-pipe that was held in the mouth, a very tricky process. From leaving school at the age of 12 he continued to learn the trade and did odd jobs of all kinds. By the age of 17 he was a fully trained metalsmith and was ready to try other things. He told ruefully of his father saying to him "We have no customers in the Yorkshire towns. Pack up some samples and spend a week up in

Yorkshire and see what you can do". At the end of the week he returned utterly despondent without taking a single order. He said to his father "I shall never make a salesman, never send me out again". "What a cruel thing to do!" he said to me.

With experience, Frank made an excellent salesman. It is not always the extrovert who does best in that job. As a young salesman he was not much impressed by the characters of the buyers that he met. Many of them were bullies who would take advantage of a young man to drive down prices. One buyer particularly upset him and he went home with very few orders because he would not reduce his prices. He thought about the encounter and began to realize that his adversary had very little knowledge about prices and values. So on his next trip to London he took a new set of patterns and a new strategy. He first asked prices that were quite unreasonably high and let himself be reluctantly beaten down to prices that were still very acceptable. The buyer gave him the biggest order that the firm had ever received and taunted Frank that he would be in trouble when he got back to Sheffield for selling at such prices! Frank was jubilant that he had learnt how to handle this kind of buyer.

Trouble with the Union

A small local trade union had a firm grip on the jobs of metalsmithing and spinning in the city. These craftsmen operated on piece-work and the union laid down a uniform piece-rate for all standard jobs. If a new design appeared it was taken to the union meeting at a local pub where it was exhaustively discussed and priced. It was useless for a manufacturer to try to be more competitive by introducing improved methods of working because no reduction of piece-rate would be contemplated by the union. New designs would be passed on to competitors through the union meeting.

Tom found his progress blocked at every turn by the union. In 1892 or '93 he gave notice to one of his men for persistent drunkenness and bad time keeping. The union demanded that the man be reinstated but Tom refused. The union then threatened to withdraw all the workers. Tom said "I'll save you the trouble. I'll give notice to all the makers-up and spinners". He then told his men what had happened and they agreed that he was right but they received their notices.

This was a courageous gamble in which Tom put on the table all that he had achieved in 20 hard years. I imagine that it was not a reckless gamble and I would guess that he must have known of some degree of dissatisfaction with the union and great loyalty among his employees. It took a lot of courage and it came off. The next day the best of the craftsmen came back to work saying that he would leave the union. Tom agreed to find him full employment at his present wage if the man would teach as many boys as Tom wished. About half the men returned on the same terms. From that day we have been a non-union company.

Frank agreed to help by going back to the bench on piece-work, with one man and three or four boys working for him. Women were engaged to do the buffing that the craftsmen had traditionally done themselves. Frank paid the man and the apprentices weekly wages and was paid piece-rate for all that the little team produced. In a short time the output was greater than it had been before and Tom was free to build the kind of business that he had always wanted. By the time he was 21 Frank had saved enough to become a partner in the firm.

By his courageous confrontation with the union Tom had won the right to manage his business; the same right has had to be won in recent years by the managements of many big British companies, the most famous being of course the National Coal Board. The transformation of these businesses has been dramatic. Just as the great National Union of Mineworkers ruined itself in recent years by its over-confident confrontation, so on a tiny scale the victory of Tom Land a hundred years earlier left the little union with unemployed men to support and consequent serious financial difficulties for itself.

Until I began to think about the history of the business, I had rather dismissed my grandfather's contribution as having been secondary to my father's. I now realize the extent of his achievement. His willingness to face difficult situations and find solutions was of the greatest importance. He got rid of his unscrupulous brothers by the highly original means of putting his business in his wife's name; he found sources of finance when he had none; he arranged a highly successful partnership with Walter Oxley; and now he released his business from the grip of the union by a bold and courageous stroke. At the same time he allowed his son Frank to earn himself a partnership in a way that brought extra cash into the firm. In all, this was an impressive performance.

In 1906 the firm becomes T. Land & Son Ltd.

By 1902 the firm was prospering sufficiently for Tom and Frank to buy out Walter Oxley; the business became T. Land and Son and in 1906 it became T. Land and Son Ltd. In 1907 Frank married my mother, Edith Mary Tym whose mother was Walter Oxley's sister, so the Oxley connection remained. My mother was an unusually well educated and well informed woman for her generation. Father called her his walking encyclopaedia. She went to Edge Hill College in Liverpool to train as a teacher. At the end of her course she had the alternatives of going on to take a degree or spending a year in France. With visions of the bright lights of Paris she opted for the latter. She wept when she discovered that she was to spend her year as répétitrice anglaise at the ecole normale at Le Puy, near Clermont Ferrand. No-one in the town spoke English, so she came home speaking fluent French with scarcely a trace of an accent. Other people's mothers seemed rather poor creatures to me as a boy!

Benefits and restraints in a non-union company

Tom was wise enough to realize that as a non-union employer he needed to rethink his attitude to craftsmen who had left the union or had been taken on as apprentices. It became an unwritten rule that a man who had served his apprenticeship at Lands would always have a job unless, of course, he misbehaved seriously. I remember Leonard Naylor who clearly never would make a decent living at piece-work and who developed a drinking problem. He was given a less demanding job cutting out metal.

Tom, and Frank after him, now learnt what could be done without a union and what restraints should be placed on a powerful bargaining position. I can report what I saw 45 years later when I joined the firm. Management and workers alike took it for granted that we were different from our competitors. Piece-rates at Lands were lower than elsewhere but the men earned more because batches were larger, working methods were more efficient and there was a tradition of working hard and effectively. There was a story that grandfather advertised for a spinner; Tom Pearson applied, but when he was told the piece-rates he said that he could not make a living at those rates. Grandfather guaranteed him £5 a week which Tom Pearson did not quite believe, but at the end of the week he had made substantially more. He was delighted and stayed on - I remember him when I was a boy.

The story of Jim Turner's visit to Canada is also worth relating. When I was at university, I spent my vacations working at the bench 'learning the trade' and Jim was my teacher. After the First World War a Canadian firm advertised in Sheffield for craftsmen and Jim decided that the wages looked attractive and he emigrated. However, when the great depression hit North America, Jim found himself out of work and starving. He wrote to 'Mr. Frank' explaining his predicament and asking for a loan of his fare back to England. Father sent him the money and gave him back his job. Jim never forgot and he brought back with him some excellent ideas that he had picked up in Canada that were put into practice to everyone's benefit.

It was Father's policy that our men were never laid off when trade was bad. Ours was a seasonal trade with orders pouring in for Christmas and then - nothing. Through February and March orders were few and our competitors laid off their workers. He always found something to make for stock that could be sold later - good selling lines like 898 tankards or 1011 teasets - and our people had a job and a wage every week of the year.

The 'model' factory that they built at Queens Road

Tom and Frank were dissatisfied with the traditional Sheffield silver-ware factory of the 19th century. I visited one or two in the 1930s - built in a hollow square three stories high around a central courtyard, with small rooms each heated in winter by a coal fire. They had a steam engine that provided the motive power to driving shafts with pulleys that operated the spinning lathes, buffing and finishing lathes and the drop stamp. A Mr. Knott approached the family, suggesting that he would like to invest in the business if his son Harry could be taken on as a partner. Tom and Frank saw the opportunity of building the factory that they had dreamed of, a model factory with big airy rooms and large windows. They found a piece of land in Queens Road, opposite the tram sheds. There they built a three-storey factory, soon raised to four storeys, which gave them 10,000 square feet of excellent accommodation. It cost just over £2,000, and was universally admired as a model of what a factory should be. The factory, as it looked more than 40 years later, is illustrated as Fig. 3.1 in Chapter 3. At the time that they moved many people warned them that they were going too far out of Sheffield. Indeed they were a long way from the small area, not much more than a quarter-mile square, in which most of the trade was concentrated, but it caused no difficulties.

As the world moved from the 19th century into the 20th century and Lands moved into their bright new factory the control of the business passed gradually from my grandfather Tom to my father Frank. Although Tom was only 22 years older than his son, he was wise enough to know that he had an exceptionally talented son and did not cling on to control of the business. My father told me that not very long after they arrived at Queens Road he was going through the accounts when he came to a rather embarrassing conclusion. At that time the business was split into two parts. He looked after the EPBM department and his father ran the EPNS department. The embarrassing discovery was that the EPBM department was making all the profit. I am sure that they looked at the position long and carefully, but there was no escaping the facts. They closed down everything but the EPBM department and the next year they had doubled the profits.

It also gave my grandfather the chance to take a much easier life at quite an early age and I have the impression that he enjoyed it. I remember him talking about "not going out until the streets are aired" and saying "it's not the early rising, it's the well spending of the day". He had worked very hard to re-establish the business that his father had squandered, now he was really content to enjoy the fruits of all that husbandry.

Frank's invention of 'machine engraving'

It was at about this time that my father invented 'machine engraving.' I often wonder whether its great success lay behind the decision to concentrate on EPBM. They were certainly running out of space in the new factory. My father made many innovations but this was the big one; I am astounded at his achievement. Before the first world war many of the teasets that we made were oval 'can shape', that is to say the body was not spun on a lathe, it was made up as a 'neck' from flat sheet metal and a flat bottom and a top were soldered on.

This was a time when the Victorian love of florid decoration still persisted and teasets were hand-engraved in patterns of scrolls, leaves and flowers. The more engraving there was on the teapot the more it was liked and the better the price could be. Some manufacturers had tried to cut the cost of engraving by making an engraved steel die and transferring the pattern to the teapot body under a press. But it did not look at all like the real thing because the decoration stood up where the metal had been pressed into the die instead of being cut out by the engraving tool.

A steel die was needed that had the decorative pattern standing out from its surface instead of being cut into it. At first this seemed impossible. One day it occurred to Frank that a pattern could be engraved on a slab of Britannia Metal and he might then be able to deposit a thick layer of electro-plated iron on the surface. If he then separated the iron from the engraved slab and he would have the die that he wanted. This process is now called electroforming.

Today the procedure is quite easy but in the early years of the twentieth century it was considered impossible. Frank went to a series of lectures on electro-plating at the University of Sheffield but he only learnt that no process of electro-plating iron was known which would produce deposits more than a few thousandths of an inch thick. Thicker deposits just peeled off. He tried other metals but they were too soft. So the idea was put on one side but not abandoned.

One day a man called at the works who had worked in America. He had a notebook full of ideas that he had picked up there that he wanted to sell. The only idea that appealed to Frank was a process for electro-depositing iron and he paid a small sum for the information. It was a strange process in which iron was deposited from a solution of iron carbonate - a most unlikely electrolyte. He made up a solution according to the formula and tried it out but without success. Frank refused to be discouraged. He tried variations on the original composition of the bath and a wide variety of current densities until at last he discovered that with a very different composition of the electrolyte and a very low current density he could deposit iron up to one-eighth of an inch thick. He said it was so slow that it was more like a petrifying well, but it worked.

This was enormously exciting and he deposited iron on one or two engraved plates, coated with graphite to make it easy to separate the iron from the base metal. So he had at last got his dies but he soon realized that the deposited iron was very soft. So he went to discuss the problem with a Dr. Andrews who was a metallurgist and who told him how to case-harden the metal to convert the surface into hard carbon steel. More great excitement as the hardened steel plates appeared and all was ready to test.

Now a new problem turned up. Frank took his plates to a press manufacturer and they tried them out on larger and larger presses but with poor results. Only a poor impression of the engraved design was made on the metal. Finally they went to a steelworks and tried it on a ten thousand ton press but again the results were poor. A less determined man might have given up at this point but Frank persevered and in the end it occurred to him that the problem was similar to the minting of coins and medals. This was the clue that he needed and eventually he found that a coining press with a big fly-wheel attached to a vertical screw thread, gave something between a squeeze and a blow and produced a perfect impression of the engraved pattern.

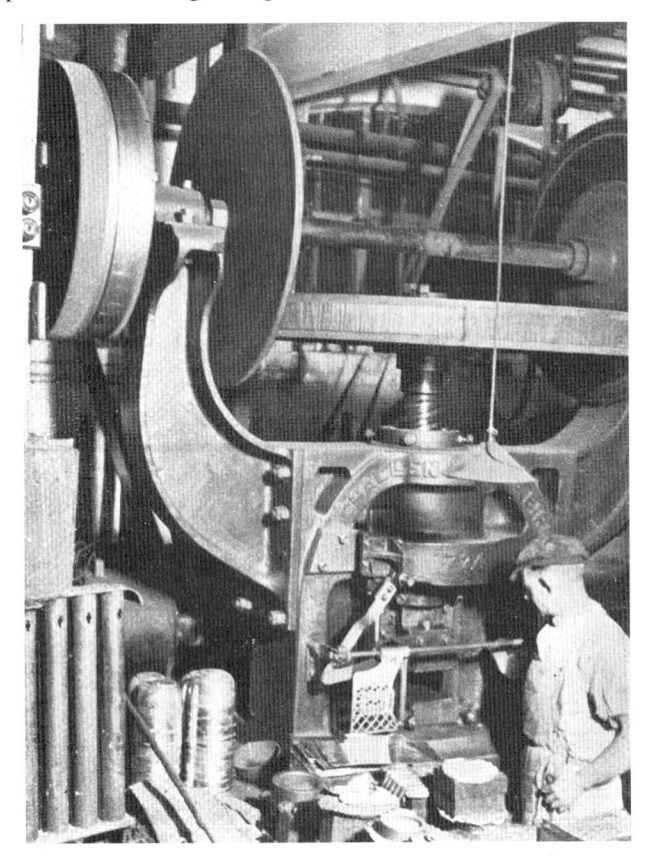

Fig. 1.6 The screw press installed in the basement at Queens Road.

The screw press, which is shown in Fig. 1.6, was installed in the basement at Queens Road alongside the two drop-stamps. The iron plating process was conducted in secret by members of the family behind locked doors. Plates were prepared, samples of teasets were made and taken up to London to show to the customers and were an instant success. Experienced buyers were unable to tell the difference between hand engraved and 'machine engraved' patterns although Frank was always perfectly honest in saying which was which. The teasets sold well and the profit from their sale quickly paid for the new equipment that had been bought.

I have never ceased to be astounded that a man who left school at 12 years old and had no scientific education could, through sheer tenacity and intelligence, carry through a development programme of this degree of originality and success, and do so while also running his business.

The First World War

The 1914-18 war was a terrible blow to this thriving business. As the war progressed more and more of the skilled men were called up and the factory was turned over to war-work. Furnaces were installed to heat blanks which were turned into fuse bodies for shells under the drop-stamps and the screw press. My father said that he did not realize what a large number a million was until he worked out that they had made a million fuse bodies during the war. The business survived.

After the war it was necessary to start again and rebuild the business, retrain workers, re-establish markets. For the first few years the demand for electro-plate far exceeded the ability of the shattered industry to supply. Frank was able to sell at prices that left a large profit margin and the process of rebuilding was in fact a very profitable one. There was also a substantial windfall. For some reason our section of the Ministry of Munitions found itself with a surplus at the end of the war and decided to distribute the surplus among its suppliers. Father often told me of his amazement when he opened the letter and saw the huge amount of the cheque; they were able to use this heaven-sent gift to finance the revival of the business.

When Harry Knott died in the great influenza epidemic of 1918 it was possible to buy the shares of the Knott family to the satisfaction of both parties. Frank built a house at Dore in 1922 and his father built a substantial bungalow at Bamford after his wife died in about 1920.

Frank fights for the survival of the business

After those first few glorious years it began to be clear that life was going to be very different in the electro-plate trade. All Frank's wonderful talents were engaged in a desperate fight to keep the business alive while our competitors went out of business one after another. Fashions had changed and would go on changing as the years went by. The days of can-shaped teasets with florid engraving were rapidly disappearing, so the machine engraved teapot was no longer a big money maker. The emphasis was on spun shapes, simple unadorned tableware; elegant shape was the only design feature that would count. Fortunately, among his talents Frank had a flair for elegant design. His cousin Harry Land was a designer at (I think) Joseph Rodgers and Frank had inherited some of the same ability to sit down and draw beautiful and original shapes. I used to watch him do it and it was marvellous to see.

Domestic servants were slowly vanishing and as they vanished the middle-class housewife became less enamoured of silver plated teasets that had to be regularly cleaned. As the years went by, the EPBM teaset was slowly squeezed out of the market by cheap EPNS from above and by chromium-plated aluminium from below.

We are shut out of the Australian market

The factory at Queens Road was called Colonial Works. This reflected the fact that Lands had carefully cultivated the export trade to Canada, South Africa, New Zealand and above all to Australia. Father used to say that he reckoned we must have sold a teaset to every family in Australia and still the orders came. It was an easy market to serve if you had the right products at the right prices because Australian suppliers bought through big exporters like Hoffnungs who bought in bulk. We had the right designs for the market and our production and prices were suited to large orders. I believe that I am correct in thinking that in the mid-twenties one third of our output went to Australia. Then the blow fell. The Australian Government decided to place a total embargo on the import of silver-plated goods to allow an Australian industry to develop. It was another crippling blow to Lands.

Survival by Boots and pewter

We survived by two means: Boots and pewter. At some time in the early twenties Boots the Chemists decided to sell silverware in all their bigger shops and they recruited two men from the Sheffield silver industry (I think from Dixons) as buyers. They knew that Lands had a reputation for quality and price and they came to Colonial Works to discuss their needs. Father saw the potential of the enquiry and we were accustomed to supplying at low prices for large quantities. The collaboration was successful for Boots and a godsend to Lands. When I joined the firm more than half our sales went to Boots; that was not comfortable but it kept us in business.

The demand for silver-plated tableware steadily declined and my father had to think furiously how he might fill the gap. He was on business in London, looking at the silverware in the shop windows as he always did, when he noticed in Liberty's windows a hammered pewter teaset. He sensed the arrival of a new fashion associated, I suppose, with the fashion for building mock-Tudor houses in the suburbs. He made up some hammered pewter teasets and found that they sold. He bought a book on old English Pewter and made up some tankards to traditional designs and they sold too.

A HUNDRED YEARS IN THE ELECTROPLATE TRADE

Fig. 1.7 Knocking spots on with a punch and a hammer.

This was all very well but these expensive items did not fit in with the Land philosophy of manufacturing in quantity at low cost and Frank began to think about the "machine-engraving" process and how to put hammer marks on pewter. At that time it was done by filling the article with a resin-based mixture and using a flat-headed punch and a small hammer to make the marks one at a time all over the surface. Fig. 1.7 shows Roland Marsh hammering a teapot body in this way. Why not punch the hammer marks on a flat steel die and then put a sheet of pewter on the die under a press? He tried it and it worked beautifully. Now he could make cheap hammered tankards.

But what about teasets? Could the same method be used on a spun-shaped teapot? Perhaps he could use a hob-die? So he designed a teapot made in two identical halves, soldered together around the middle, the shape of a grapefruit cut in two halves and put together again. A steel die was made which just fitted inside one half of the teapot and the die was covered with hammer marks. This nearly hemispherical die was then screwed into a larger hollow die like a half grapefruit, flat side down in a big pudding basin as I have shown in Fig. 1.8. The upper die was made by pouring molten metal into the lower die and the whole thing was used in the traditional way under the drop stamp that is shown in Fig. 1.9. The stamp, which is normally intended to form flat metal into rounded shapes, was now used simply to knock spots on a spun blank of pewter. The hammer marks came up most successfully.

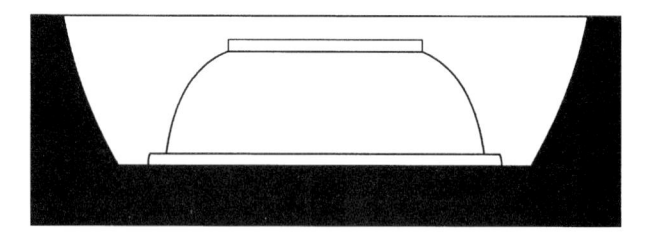

Fig. 1.8 A hob die for knocking hammer marks on one half of a teapot body.

Fig. 1.9 A drop stamp at Queens Road.

Thus was born the 1011 teaset which Father took to Boots to see if they could sell it. They jumped at the idea and together they launched cheap machine-hammered teasets onto the market. The success was immediate and Frank had found a replacement for the lost Australian market and the declining demand for silver-plated tableware. Necessity is indeed the mother of invention; but it needs a touch of business genius to bring the invention into the world as successfully as this.

Concentrate and simplify

Meanwhile the electroplate trade was slowly and steadily dying and our competitors were disappearing every year. All the genius in the world could only keep us alive and profitable; there was no thought of growth, indeed our employees slowly declined in numbers from over 100 to about 80, but the business survived and was profitable.

I read in the paper recently of an Indian businessman who was saving small-to-medium businesses in the Midlands by cutting their overhead expenses drastically and simplifying everything. He should have seen the simplicity of the operation at Lands! Father was Managing Director, Works Manager, Product Development Manager and Designer and the entire sales force himself. We had one girl in the office who typed letters and invoices and kept the books, and there was Charlie Barker who was 'getting-up orders', i.e. the progress function. Everyone else was making things or packing things. We had a manufacturers' representative in London who sold our pewter alongside other manufacturers' products to smaller customers. That was all. Father's younger brother Harold looked after the machinery and electrical equipment.

The control of costs and prices was equally simple. Father designed perhaps a hundred new lines every year. Each was sketched in the design book and alongside each sketch he recorded the costs - weight and cost of metal and of silver, cost of plastic handle and knob, spinning and assembling costs (both piece-work) and so on. These exact amounts represented about three quarters of the total cost of the article. The sum was then doubled and that was a starting point for the selling price. Father would hold up this finished sample and say "Now what could I get for that?" Sometimes he decided he would get a bit more than double the "cost". If the quantities were large he might be quite content to get substantially less.

At the year-end Father would look at the bank account and see how much we could take out as additional salaries. Since the business was not growing there was no need for additional working capital and all the profit could be paid out. Having decided in this way how much profit he could declare for the year he decided the value of the stock that he would need to declare to balance the books. He then went round with a little red book writing down the value of the stock on the shelves and in the showroom until he had the total that he thought was about right and then he stopped. There was always a large hidden reserve of undeclared stock - sheets of silver, ingots of tin, finished goods. The whole process was very simple, very quick, perfectly adequate and, above all, safe and conservative. There was always money in the bank.

By simplifying the organization in these ways and by concentrating on a small number of large customers, Lands were able to offer products of excellent design and finish at prices that left the competition standing and returned a good profit year after year. In a contracting, cut-throat market it was a superb achievement.

Don't go into the plate trade, Tom.

As a boy I had no doubts that I wanted to join the family business. I was not encouraged by my father, who was having to struggle and fight every inch of the way. "Don't come into the plate trade", he said, "go into something to eat or something to wear that people always need." But it all sounded interesting and challenging; that was the life for me, although I had the sense to doubt if I would ever be as good at it as my father.

Father decided that if I really wanted to join him in the family business I would need to leave school at 16 and learn the trade thoroughly. In the sixth form I was studying mathematics, physics and chemistry and when I was in my second year the Headmaster wrote to father saying he thought that I might win a scholarship to Cambridge. Father was doubtful but went to see the Headmaster and was persuaded to let me sit for the examination. In the higher school certificate examination (now A levels), I had distinctions in mathematics and physics and was awarded a State Scholarship and a County Major Scholarship to go to Cambridge. Father was rather proud and said "Well, I suppose you will have to go." It proved to be a good thing that I did. But a few months after I had won my scholarship the Government decided to apply a means test to State Scholarships. Instead of paying my own way, I had to rely on my father to meet the cost of my university education. I remember being very angry; I recorded every penny I spent in a little book - for my own peace of mind.

Cambridge - and learning a trade

The night before I went up to Cambridge I changed my mind about the subjects I would study. I had decided that the subject most likely to be useful at the works would be chemistry; but the subjects that I really enjoyed were mathematics and physics. On that night one of the masters at school dropped in to wish me luck and I talked to him about my choice of subject. He advised me to read the subjects that interested me most, so when I arrived at Emmanuel College I switched to Part 1 Mathematics with a view to reading Part 2 Physics in my second and third years. This decision changed the whole future of the business.

When I went to Cambridge in 1932 I was keenly aware that my time there was a luxury, a concession to my deep interest in physics at that time when the structure of the atom itself was being uncovered. I enjoyed every minute of it, but the vacations were not devoted to revision and study. I went down to the works every morning and got on with the serious business of learning all about the business that all too soon I would have to manage on behalf of the family and myself. I came down from Cambridge in 1935 with a respectable degree in physics. Working at the bench during the vacations had also given me sufficient practical experience in the trade. That experience cut down to size any feelings of superiority that I might have developed at university. It was a salutary experience to sit all day among the metalsmiths on a three-legged stool, trying vainly to solder a seam with tin solder in a pewter tankard body while all those around me were doing it with perfect ease - and to do the same thing every day for a week. I have a profound respect for craftsmen.

Learning from Father

In 1935 my father was 60, still active and impressively competent. I knew that I would have to learn fast to be ready to take over from him. It was often a frustrating experience. There was no job that I could make my own and get my teeth into and Father was not very good at delegating. His efficient ultra-simple organization was not an easy place to learn. Nevertheless I learned a lot just working beside him. I attended a course of lectures at Sheffield University on business management, given by T. G. Rose, after which I began to prepare monthly accounts. They did not contribute much to the success of the business at the time but they laid the foundation of financial control for later years.

I learnt to sell when we took our bags of new samples up to London and engaged a room at the Manchester Hotel in Aldersgate Street. I remember being desperately nervous when I first went on my own to Boots, but they were very kind. I learnt to be Works Manager when Father went on a fortnight's holiday and tried so hard that I was quite knackered when he came back. I tried my hand at designing and attended design classes at the School of Art; but when I compared my efforts with Father's the comparison was pitiful. I instituted proper chemical analysis of the plating vats and felt more at home, but I never contemplated buying a fume cupboard. When I boiled off the deadly hydrocyanic acid I opened the window wide and held my breath when I was in the room. We didn't waste money! When the typist was on holiday I did the typing - there wasn't much, just the invoices and a few brief letters. One way and another I learnt a lot.

In 1938 Boots asked us to provide them with some pictures of the processes involved in making pewter and EPBM and to prepare a booklet so that their staff could learn about the craftsmanship in the trade. I took all the pictures myself and prepared the booklet. Large photographs were displayed in the principal Boots shops for the customers to see. I was fortunate to find recently that a friend had kept a copy of this booklet and I have used several of them as illustrations in the text of this chapter. A recent television programme showed the same processes being carried out 50 years later exactly as we did them in 1938. Visitors to the works were always entranced to see the many wonderful skills in use. I thought that you might like to see the rest of them so I have grouped them together in Figs. 1.10 and 1.11.

Fig. 1.10a
Casting a hollow teapot handle.
The molten pewter is poured into the
brass mould, then poured straight out
again, leaving a hollow casting.

Fig. 1.10b
George Calvert pouring metal
into an ingot mould.

One thing that I learnt in my first four years was that the survival of the business was getting more difficult. EPBM was steadily losing ground to cheap EPNS and chromium-plated aluminium. I was not impressed with pewter as a metal for teapots, it was too soft and slowly lost its shape at the temperature of hot tea. I was casting around for new products - perhaps stainless steel? What about the new process of anodising, was there anything for us there? Could silver be protected from tarnishing? A new research association for the silver trade was trying out some new ideas in this field and I tried to duplicate their results, with no success.

Another war

My generation grew up knowing the horror of the First World War and uncomfortably aware of the gathering clouds of the Second. By early 1939 there was talk of conscription and I joined the Territorial Army with some of my friends so that I could have some choice of where I would fight. I joined the Artillery. The government made a register of all physicists and I wrote down my qualifications and sent them off. Business got worse as war approached. In August, I returned from Territorial Army camp to hear that my father had been talking to his friend and neighbour Fred Lea, who was Professor of Engineering at Sheffield University, and who was asking about me. "He mustn't waste his talents as a gunner" said Fred Lea, "Physicists are going to be desperately needed in wartime. Tell him to go and see Mr. Oliver who is Director of Research at Jessops and mention my name. Oliver is making a name for himself in the steel industry". I went to see him and Mr. Oliver offered me a job on the spot; I was to take over the Pyrometry Department. It was a wonderful break for me and very soon I knew that this was the thing that I was good at, the thing that I would like to do for the rest of my life.

Fig.1.11a Hand burnishing.

Fig. 1.11b Making-up.

Fig.1.11c Engraving.

Fig. 1.11d Polishing.

CHAPTER 2
MY SEVEN YEARS AT JESSOPS
1939 to 1946

Wm. Jessop & Sons Ltd.

Jessops was one of the smaller Sheffield steelworks, employing about 2000 people, located at the end of Brightside Lane. When I passed that way recently the demolition men were knocking down the office block. Once a family firm, it was then part of the BSA group. They did a bit of everything so I got a very wide experience. They had a small 20 ton open hearth melting furnace and a ridiculously small one as well. They had three arc furnaces (10 ton capacity) and two 'electric crucible furnaces' that were high frequency induction furnaces for making magnet steels and tool steels. They even had some old crucible furnaces for tool steel, some of the last in Sheffield. There was a forge, a foundry, a small rolling mill, the magnet shop (this was good) and the file shop. Looking back it is clear that everything except the magnet shop was going to be on too small a scale to be profitable in the post-war world.

Donald Oliver was head of the Research Department, a physicist of about 35 who had worked at the National Physical Laboratory, full of charm, kindness and a fair streak of intellectual arrogance, keen to know all the right people and mix with the intellectual nobs, which was no bad thing at all. He had gathered a team of first class young graduates around him many of whom became heads of businesses after they left Jessops; one became Managing Director of Jessops. We were given good projects that took us onto the right technical committees and into important new developments; Geoff Harris was working on steels for the secret Whittle Jet Engine, Dennis Hadfield was developing magnets for radar. I was given the new British invention of the 'quick immersion' technique for liquid steel temperature measurement.

My job at Jessops

Our present business grew directly out of my work at Jessops. Indeed it was virtually a single career, interrupted only by my short period at BSA Group Research Centre which Donald Oliver also controlled at the end of the war. I must therefore explain in some detail what I did.

My basic job was to run the pyrometry department that had the responsibility of keeping all the temperature measuring instruments in good working order. I was given lads to help me. They would come from school for a year or two until they were called up into the services and I would then get a replacement. I had some excellent boys including three who later joined me at Land Pyrometers. The instruments that we serviced were of two kinds. The temperatures of the heat treatment furnaces were measured by thermocouples. A thermocouple consists of a pair of wires of different heat resisting metals, welded together at one end. The wires of our thermocouples were kept apart by twin-hole ceramic insulators (Fig. 2.1) and protected from the furnace atmosphere by a metal or ceramic sheath. The wires produced a small electric voltage that depended on the temperature of the hot junction and the compositions of the two wires. They were connected through a terminal head and special cable to a meter (then usually a galvanometer) graduated in degrees C. The thermocouple wires deteriorated at the high temperature; it was my job to check their accuracy and repair or replace them as necessary.

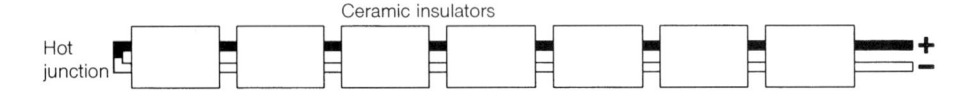

Fig. 2.1 An industrial thermocouple.

The other instruments were entirely different. Portable optical pyrometers measure the temperature of a red hot surface by measuring the brightness of the red light that it emits. An operator looks at the hot object through a red filter in a small telescope. He sees the hot surface and, superimposed on it, the filament of a lamp located in the telescope. The filament can be made to look darker or brighter than the hot body by varying the current that was passed through the filament. The instrument is called a disappearing filament pyrometer because the filament disappears when its brightness is exactly the same as that of the hot body. When the filament disappears the current through the filament is measured by a meter that is built into the instrument and is calibrated in temperature. It was my job to check the accuracy of these pyrometers. As I carried out these routine tasks I learnt the advantages and limitations of all the available instruments and components and I developed ideas for their improvement that I was able to put into practice later in my own business.

Measuring the temperature of liquid steel

As well as this routine work, I was given the specific job of developing liquid steel temperature measurement. For many years steel makers had tried without success to measure the temperature of the liquid steel in furnaces and ladles. In the years just before the war the Iron and Steel Institute had set up the Liquid Steel Temperature Sub-Committee to tackle this important and difficult problem and they had enlisted the help of the National Physical Laboratory. Dr. F.H. Schofield, who was head of the relevant section of the NPL, and his assistant Mr. A. Grace had found a solution to the problem. They had provided a number of instruments to a few Sheffield steelworks, including Jessops, to try in their furnaces.

The method that Schofield and Grace had devised was simple and ingenious. They used a platinum rhodium thermocouple, as others had done before. But previous attempts had failed because nobody had found a sheath to protect the thermocouple that would withstand the temperature of the steel and the corrosive action of the slag without cracking from the thermal shock of immersion in the liquid metal. The only hope was to use a fused silica protection tube; but silica, which is immune to thermal shock, softens rapidly at steel-making temperatures so it was discarded as unsuitable. Schofield and Grace decided to try a small thin silica protection tube and to leave it in the steel for only just long enough (5 to 10 seconds) for the thermocouple wire to reach the temperature of the steel. The silica tube could be used once but it was not expensive. The method worked well and at last it was possible to measure the temperature of liquid steel. But the method was not being used to contol the melting process in the steel works.

Donald Oliver was determined to get that further step taken and he gave me the task of developing the technique to the point where it could be used with confidence and convenience. There was much to be done both in the design of the thermocouple and in the temperature indication, and the problems were not solved quickly. Eventually I designed two kinds of thermocouple unit that could be picked up by the furnaceman and put in the steel and could then be quickly fitted with a new silica dipping tube ready for the next dip.

Fig. 2.2 A thermocouple for measuring the temperature of liquid steel in an induction furnace at Jessops.

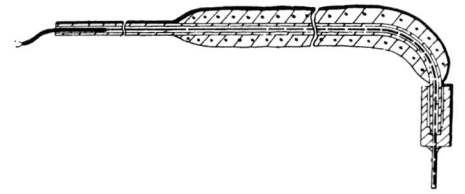

Fig. 2.3 A portable pyrometer for measurements in arc furnaces.

One was designed for our arc furnaces and our 20 ton open hearth furnace (a small one); the other was suitable for high frequency induction furnaces and small ladles. The simpler one for induction furnaces, Fig. 2.2, used a modified drill chuck to grip the disposable silica tube. The thermocouple used in the arc furnace, Fig. 2.3, had a long steel tube to reach into the white-hot furnace with a graphite end-block to protect the immersed end from the slag and the liquid metal. The tube itself was insulated from the furnace heat by a thick coating of refractory cement, reinforced by a coil of steel wire. This coating was invented under pressure of time. Donald Oliver had promised someone at a neighbouring steel-works to let them borrow a pyrometer by a certain date and we just had to invent something that worked within the promised time, which we did. This was effective project management.

Developing a special recorder for the job

Next I turned my thoughts to the measuring instrument. The instrument that was then being used was a portable, hand operated potentiometer which measured the voltage generated by the thermocouple. It was barely fast enough for the job and we had to have a conversion table to convert millivolts to degrees C. It needed a highly skilled operator on the potentiometer, and a furnaceman dipping the thermocouple. This was not a production tool.

Electronic potentiometers were not then available in England and it was impossible to buy a temperature recorder that was fast enough and accurate enough for this measurement. But one day we had a visit from Mr. D.C. Gall, Managing Director of H. Tinsley and Co. Ltd., the premier suppliers of high class laboratory potentiometers in the U.K. He brought with him an Austrian refugee called Fritz Steghart who had arrived in England from Germany with no money, a useful introduction, and an idea. He had been working at Siemens in Germany on a fast galvanometer amplifier which he had now perfected for Mr. Gall and they were looking for an application. Needless to say we had one and in due course Fritz brought along an amplifier and a recorder that met my specification for the liquid steel temperature job. I soon decided to fit a switch that would turn on the chart motor when the temperature was above 1400°C and a time switch that sounded a klaxon horn after 10 seconds.

The temperature recorder that we used is illustrated in Fig. 2.4 and a length of chart paper with a series of records of measurements is shown in Fig. 2.5. At last we had a liquid steel temperature measuring system that could be used by the melting shop, the first in the world, and the Jessops melting shop began to operate their furnaces on the basis of accurately measured temperatures. Before long other British steel works were buying Tinsley recorders and producing thermocouples to suit their own local conditions.

Fig. 2.4
The world's first liquid steel temperature recorder.

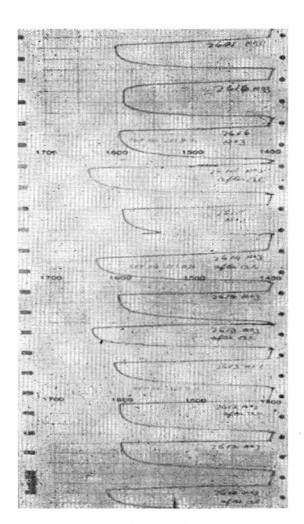

Fig. 2.5
The 3° inch wide chart showing several records of 'dips' made at Jessops.

Exploring the temperature variations in a furnace

The next thing was to find out whether a single measurement at one point in the furnace or a ladle was sufficiently representative of the temperature of the whole of the liquid metal. I made a thorough survey of all our furnaces to determine the temperature gradients at different times during the steelmaking cycle. These were extremely important measurements and they created quite a stir when we reported them to the Liquid Steel Temperature Sub-Committee for publication in the Journal of the Iron & Steel Institute. They showed that there were quite large gradients at certain times in arc furnaces but that with certain precautions the results were acceptable. The famous Dr. Hatfield of Firth Browns, the most renowned and redoubtable figure in steel technology at the time, immediately instigated a similar survey in the Firth Brown furnaces so that he could publish a similar paper in the same issue of the Journal as ours!

At the same time David Manterfield was taking measurements in the larger open hearth furnaces at Steel Peach and Tozer and David Cresswell was doing work at Hadfields. We all met and exchanged experiences at the meetings of the Liquid Steel Temperature Sub-Committee. In a friendly spirit of rivalry and co-operation we got the quick immersion method operating successfully and eventually accepted by the managements of all the Sheffield steelworks.

Making a few thermocouples at Queens Road

I wrote several papers and people from other steelworks would come to Jessops to see the equipment that we were using. The next questions would be whether it would be possible for Mr. Land to make up one or two thermocouples for them to try. One day Donald Oliver said to me that this was getting to be a bit too much and he had been wondering whether we had anybody at T. Land and Son who could make the thermocouples for these people. So it came about that we began to make liquid steel thermocouples at Queens Road. The largest order that we had resulted from a visit that Donald Oliver made to America. He arranged for us to ship three sets of thermocouples out to two American plants and one Canadian plant. It is clear from the early post-war literature on liquid steel temperature that the Americans based their thermocouples on my designs but modified them to suit their rather different conditions. This work that I did at Jessops was later to form the basis of the business that became Land Pyrometers.

Designing a better radiation pyrometer for the open hearth furnace

While I was at Jessops I was also working on radiation thermometry and that work would lead on to Land Infrared. It began with practical difficulties in our open-hearth melting furnace. A steel melting furnace is a room-sized chamber that has to be not just red-hot, but white-hot. The furnace chamber is so bright that it is dazzling; it is impossible to see anything in the furnace without wearing dark glasses. The furnaces are lined with special refractory bricks that can withstand these extraordinary temperatures. The roof of our open-hearth furnace was made of silica bricks. If the roof got a bit too hot it began to drip and form stalactites and soon it would need re-building - a very expensive job. Observers with optical pyrometers, therefore, had the job of checking the roof temperature from time to time, but they were not always around when things went wrong.

Some Sheffield steelworks measured the temperature of their furnace roofs continuously with 'total radiation pyrometers'. Such pyrometers measure not only the brightness of the light from the roof but also the radiant heat. Some used Foster pyrometers; I borrowed one to test and found it dreadful. I felt sure that I could design something better than that.

I had found a paper by Larsen and Shenk who had designed a roof pyrometer in America that used selenium photoelectric cells to measure the brightness and hence the temperature of the furnace roof. These selenium cells were the size and shape of today's two pence piece. They were made of iron and coated on one side with a layer of selenium, covered in turn by a very thin coating of gold. They were used at that time in photographic exposure meters and our friends at the National Physical Laboratory at Teddington were experimenting with them for temperature measurement. It seemed a good idea to

MY SEVEN YEARS AT JESSOPS

get hold of some of these cells to test their properties and see whether I might use one in a pyrometer for the Jessop furnace.

I began to be most enthusiastic when I made my measurements in the laboratory and plotted the results on the largest piece of semi-logarithmic graph paper that I could find. I saw the results falling with a precision within a degree or two of a straight line whose slope I soon realized was a measure of the wavelength of the red light that the cell was measuring. The speed of response was phenomenal. I decided that I could find many uses for these cells. I built a roof pyrometer for our open hearth melting furnace, Fig. 2.6, and another pyrometer that measured the temperature of magnet alloys as they were melted in a high-frequency induction furnace. I published a paper describing them and another that described an experiment with the roof pyrometer that exploited its very fast response.

Fig. 2.6 The roof pyrometer that I built at Jessops.

Measuring hot surfaces below red heat - in cold surroundings

This work led me on to consider methods of measuring lower temperatures using radiation thermometers and doing so with greater precision than had previously been achieved. The need for such measurements turned up in the work of another sub-committee, the Foundry Steel Temperature Sub-Committee, of which I was secretary. There was no known method of doing this with acceptable accuracy.

When a surface is red hot its temperature can be determined by measuring the brightness of the red light that it emits. If it is not hot enough to emit red light it is still possible to measure its temperature by measuring the intensity of the invisible infrared radiation that it emits - otherwise known as radiant heat. There is just one snag which applies to both red light and infrared radiation, but more seriously to the infrared. I must explain the difficulty as simply as I can.

First I must explain that the red light that we see coming from a red hot body is not just a surface phenomenon. The whole bulk of the body is full of red light and the brightness and colour of the light within the hot body are determined only by the body's temperature. This internal luminosity is the perfect means of measuring the temperature. The snag is that the light has to get out before it can be measured. If the surface were perfectly black (i.e. non-reflecting) all the light would pass through the surface and could be measured to give the true temperature. But all real surfaces are reflective and some of the light does not escape through the surface. The degree of reflectivity can only be estimated, so an element of uncertainty is always present. The potential error is much more serious when infrared radiation is used instead of light.

The committee was keen to find how to eliminate this uncertainty in the measurement and we had a post-graduate student finding out what was known about the emissivities of metals and oxides. There is no uncertainty if the radiation is measured in a deep cavity; this is essentially because the hole is "black" or non-reflecting. The radiation emitted from a small hole in a uniform temperature enclosure is the full internal radiation and is called black-body radiation.

I patent the idea of a pyrometer with a hemispherical mirror attached

One evening as I was getting ready for bed and this problem was turning over in my mind, it occurred to me that if a mirror were placed over a hot surface the hot surface would be surrounded by its own reflection in the mirror. The space between the hot surface and mirror would be equivalent to a uniform temperature enclosure and the radiation emerging from a small hole in the mirror would be very nearly the full black-body radiation and dependent only on the temperature of the hot surface. I soon realized that the mirror should be hemispherical like the skin of half a grapefruit with a little hole at the apex of the mirror as I have shown in Fig. 2.7. I took out a patent on the idea and tried it out. It certainly looked promising and I reported the results to the committee. But other things became more urgent and it was a few years before I could return to my invention. It was later to become the Land Surface Pyrometer, but that is a story for Chapter 5.

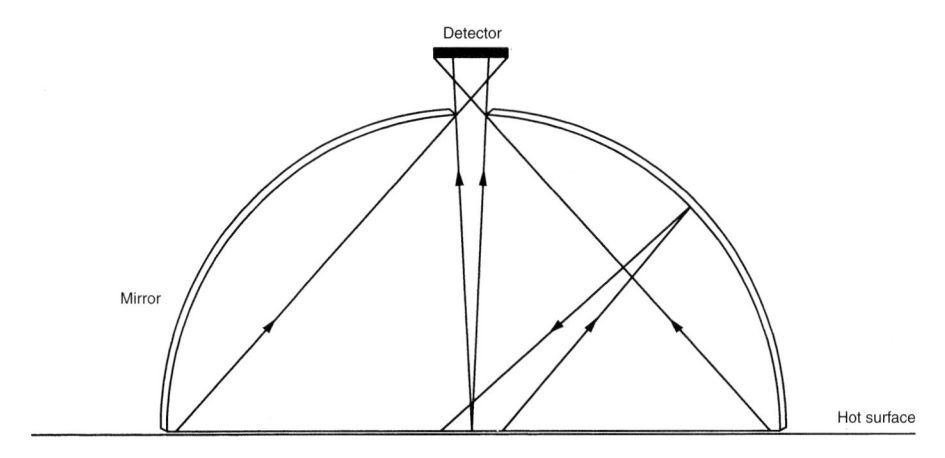

Fig. 2.7 My idea for a surface pyrometer using a reflecting hemisphere.

Incidentally, it was while I was working at Jessops that I met the girl I married. Audrey Mennie was a teacher, daughter of a teacher in Rotherham. Her grandfather had been principal of a very large school in Liverpool. She was nice-looking with dark brown hair and pale blue eyes, with dark arched eyebrows that made her look just a bit surprised. She was a beautiful dancer, athletic, intelligent and easy to get on with. We were married on 5th June 1943 at Rotherham Parish Church and lived first in Rotherham, which was convenient for her teaching at Greasbrough and my work in Brightside. I spent the next few years discovering what a treasure I had acquired - loyal, affectionate, strong-minded, wise. Our first daughter Celia was born on 29 March 1944.

Donald Oliver starts up the BSA Group Research Centre, which I join

Wm. Jessop and Sons was part of the BSA Group which also included BSA Tools, BSA Motorcycles and Daimler Cars, who also made motor buses. The Group decided in 1944 that they should have a central research department and Donald Oliver was persuaded very reluctantly to run it as well as the Jessops research department. They acquired Greystones Hall in Ecclesall, Sheffield and fitted it out as a research centre. Donald Oliver asked me to be responsible for the day-to-day management of the Centre, but this did not extend to any policy decisions.

In my opinion Greystones was at that time a perfect example of how not to run a research department. This was surprising because the Jessop research department was chaotic but highly effective. At Greystones we would be given a project, we would write a report when it was completed and that was the end. We rarely had contact with the companies in the group nor did we know what had happened to our reports. Donald Oliver was rarely around, he was usually at Jessops or off on his travels.

I go to Power Jets and learn to design a small jet engine

Nevertheless I was given one job that was enormously challenging and interesting. We had a consultant (Sir Frank Smith) who told Daimler, quite rightly, that they should learn all they could about gas turbines. Such engines were beginning to be used in the new jet fighter aircraft, and they might be useful in heavy transport vehicles such as motor buses and lorries. The knowledge about jet engines was, of course, a military secret known only to the RAF and Rolls Royce who were making the engines. But Jessops were making turbine discs of special heat resisting steel for Rolls Royce, so Donald Oliver had excellent contacts. He managed to get permission for me to attend a four-week course at Power Jets at Lutterworth on the design of gas turbines. I was then to come back and do a design study for a 120 H.P. engine for a motor bus.

I came back with a set of notes that I had taken during the course (we were given nothing in writing) from which I wrote a report on how to design an engine. I acquired a drawing board and a supply of paper and set about the job. I calculated all the gas velocities and temperatures through the compressor and the two-stage turbine and all the profiles of the turbine and compressor blades. Of course we had no electronic calculators, so the intricate calculations had to be done on a slide rule. I then made drawings to show how it would work out in practice. I concluded that a small gas turbine might be successful if the efficiencies of the compressor and turbine were equally good in the scaled-down model. But it would require a very large heat exchanger if the efficiency were to be acceptable. The Rover Motor Company later made a turbine for a car that was remarkably similar to my design. I was right to be cautious in my recommendations. The small gas turbine was not a commercial proposition.

CHAPTER 3
THE FOUNDING OF LAND PYROMETERS
1947 to 1963

I have to decide my future career

When the war ended, Donald Oliver asked me if I intended to stay with him at Greystones Hall or whether I would be returning to the family business. My father and my uncle asked the same question. It was decision time but the decision was not easy to make. I knew that my talents lay not with the business that my father and grandfather had built, but in the field of applied physics in which I had been so happy and successful at Jessops. On the other hand I knew that my parents and other family members were dependent on the business. Their careful savings had been invested chiefly in government securities whose value had largely been lost during the war. This business was also my inheritance which I was most reluctant to abandon and business was in my blood.

Looking back today on my years in the family business, I realize that this conflict between businessman and scientist has always affected my career. It was to be a danger, giving the business a tendency to be driven by technology. I have always had a weakness for following some fascinating line of mathematical investigation and letting the business roll along on its own. It has also been a strength, driving me to delegate responsibility to others so that I could follow my scientific interests for a while without endangering the business. On balance I think that this tension in my mind has been beneficial. It has produced a business based on very good science while my willingness to delegate has developed other people's talents and has given us a business that has outlived my personal involvement.

While I was turning the question of my future career over and over in my mind my father had a visit from Bert Walker, an acquaintance at the church. His electro-plate business had folded up during the war and he had taken a job as a book-keeper at the Amalgams Company. He told Father what a fine, profitable business it was. "Much better than the plate trade", he told Father "you should see the profit margins that they make."

I set out to build an industrial instrument company - cautiously

So Father's mind began to move on much the same lines as mine was taking. I began to think that I might be able to build an industrial instrument company, but I would need to start with something simple and profitable. I might develop my ideas about instrumentation into something practicable within this profitable environment. I knew the Amalgams Company well. I had bought from them all the spare parts and equipment that I needed to service and repair the thermocouples at Jessops. They had no real competitors. We might be able to start up a business in the same line, making use of my knowledge and my contacts in the steel industry. In the end we decided to have a go. I started to work part-time at Queens Road in August 1946 and I left BSA at the end of the year.

We engage Roy Marsh

Among the friends with whom I had travelled to school at Chesterfield Grammar School from Dore and Totley station was Roy Marsh. The Marshes moved to Sheffield from Leicester in the nineteen twenties. Mr. Marsh was a commercial traveller who represented a firm of confectionery manufacturers. They had squeezed a hard tennis court into their garden and I often went across from Dore to Heatherfield to see Roy and his parents and have a game of tennis.

When Roy had taken his School Certificate it was thought that he had developed a touch of tuberculosis. The doctor recommended an outdoor life, so instead of going into the sixth form he joined the merchant navy, where he travelled the world, took his master's certificate and then transferred to the Royal Navy. When war broke out he was second in command of a British submarine. We always kept in touch and saw each other when he was at home on leave.

Early in the war, off the coast of Italy, Roy's submarine encountered the Italian navy. It was such a close encounter that one of the Italian ships scraped the hull of the submarine and caused a certain amount of damage. The Captain panicked and decided to surface and surrender his ship. Roy was aware that the submarine was quite seaworthy and indignantly protested that they should not surrender, but to no avail. He spent the rest of the war as a prisoner of war in Italy, where he learnt to speak Italian. After the war the Captain knew that he faced a court martial with Roy as a principal witness. He was well connected and succeeded in having Roy court-martialled for insubordination before his own trial took place. Roy was dismissed from the service. Although the Captain was later found guilty of surrendering his ship that was not much consolation for Roy.

When I heard of this shocking miscarriage of justice I realized that we could offer Roy more than sympathy; we could offer him a job. We talked it over with him and he was delighted to accept my suggestion that he should join us as a salesman for our new venture in pyrometer supplies. He went on to become sales manager and a director of Land Pyrometers. He was a good friend, an excellent salesman and an enthusiastic colleague.

THE FOUNDING OF LAND PYROMETERS 43

Roy was allowed to work in the pyrometry department at Jessops for a few months to get an understanding of the pyrometry business. He then came to join me at Queens Road and we recruited a man to look after the stores and a girl to do the typing. We had ordered some ceramic insulators and protection tubes, thermocouple wires and other spares from the manufacturers and when these arrived we were in business. The new business and its three employees occupied the right-hand corner of the top floor of the factory (Fig. 3.1, below).

Fig. 3.1 A view of Colonial Works, Queens Road about 1950.

A business like the Amalgams Company

The Amalgams Company did indeed have a good, well-run business. They did a substantial amount of manufacturing but the core of their business was re-sale. The steelworks all over Britain bought their requirements of pyrometer spares from them. They, in turn, bought protection tubes and insulators from the Morgan Crucible Company and the Thermal Syndicate, base metal thermocouple wires from Hoskins, rare metal thermocouple wire from Johnson Matthey and Co and so on. They received a 25%

resale discount on everything except rare metal thermocouple wires.

There was one weakness in their position. At the end of the war the supply of most of these items was barely sufficient to meet the demand. So when we began to place large orders with their suppliers, Amalgams began to have empty shelves. With hard work by Roy and my good connections with people in charge of the pyrometry departments we soon began to capture some of the market.

It was not quite so easy to get a share of the silica dipping tube business. In liquid steel temperature measurement the platinum thermocouple was protected from the liquid steel by a small silica tube that was used once and then thrown away. There was a lot of business to be done and, as I felt that I had done as much as anybody to create the market, I was determined to have part of that business. Unfortunately there was only one manufacturer in the U.K., the Thermal Syndicate at Wallsend-on-Tyne, and they had given the Amalgams Company the sole right to sell dipping tubes.

I was not prepared to accept this situation. I decided to buy lengths of open-ended tubing from the Thermal Syndicate and I engaged girls to seal the ends with an oxy-acetylene torch. We then sold the tubes a bit cheaper than the standard prices of dipping tubes. A little later we discovered that the French firm of Quartz et Silice had started to manufacture dipping tubes. I suggested to them that their gentlemen's agreement with Thermal Syndicate not to sell in each other's territories might be reconsidered and I let it be known at Wallsend-on-Tyne that discussions were proceeding. Quite soon we and the Amalgams Company became joint sole distributors! The market was growing rapidly and there was room for both of us. For many years silica dipping tubes were our biggest selling line.

We soon began to manufacture or sell all the equipment needed to measure the temperature of liquid steel and our first big order came from France. During the war the British Steel industry developed liquid steel temperature measurement ahead of the rest of the world. Soon after we started in business a delegation from the newly established French steel research institute IRSID visited Britain to ensure that the French Steel industry would be brought up to date in this field. They were recommended to come to us and we sold them a large batch of immersion thermocouples and a number of Tinsley recorders. We also supplied sufficient silica dipping tubes and other spares to get them started. 'Roy Marsh followed up the order and in the next few years we had quite a good business with the French steelworks.

The new business grows fast

For the first three years we ran the new business as a department of T. Land and Son Ltd, alongside the old pewter and electro-plate business. The new 'Instrument Department' quickly overtook the old business as shown in the following table.

YEAR	ELECTROPLATE & PEWTER	INSTRUMENTS
1947/48	£24.0k	£21.2k
1948/49	£28.8k	£27.4k
1949/50	£23.7k	£38.6k

As the business grew we engaged new people, including Jeff Blake, who had been with me at Jessops and John McHenry who had been in charge of the pyrometry department at Edgar Allens. We could not afford to buy cars for the salesmen, they had to use their own; but we did buy a delivery van. Fig. 3.1 shows the van standing outside the factory in Queens Road.

My cousin Eric Land joins the family business

My cousin Eric Land, son of father's younger brother Harold, was 12 years younger than me and had been a radar mechanic in the Royal Navy during the war. When he was demobilized his parents were keen that he should join the firm. Father was not enthusiastic but I thought that there would be trouble in the family if I did not give him a chance to show what he could do. So I wrote to him and invited him to join us.

I suggested that he should first complete his education. Father and mother offered to pay for him to go to Cambridge but that was neither acceptable nor practicable and he went to Rotherham Technical College to take an external BSc from London University. He did not do too well in his first year's examinations. The business was developing rapidly and I was filling up the key positions with good people. I could foresee family problems, so I advised him to give up his studies and come and join us immediately. He came to join us early in 1950. It was fortunate for me that he turned out to be a much more competent man than his father.

Eric's relationship with me was bedevilled by family history which I had better explain because otherwise many things would be incomprehensible. Harold was 18 years younger than my father and as he grew up he became a source of considerable anxiety to his parents. His upbringing was utterly different from that of my father who left school at 12 to learn the trade. Harold was adored by his elder sister Beatrice, who was about 15 when he was born and who largely devoted herself to bringing him up. He had a good education and there was money to spend on him. In her home Beatrice had a picture of the young Harold riding a horse.

While he was still at school he had a nervous breakdown and Grandfather was at a loss to know what to do with him. He was interested in electrical engineering and Frank thought that he should have made a career where his interests lay. But Grandfather was aware that Harold never seemed to make a success of anything and he decided that he should go to the works where Frank would look after him. I understand how he must have felt.

The arrangement was a disaster; heaven knows whether any other arrangement would have been better. Harold could not be given any responsible job other than looking after the machinery and electrical equipment which he did quite well. Frank was often exasperated with him and told him so, rather publicly. Beatrice believed that Frank treated Harold badly and that her boy had a very poor deal. Eric was brought up in that belief and it was a big shock to him when he came to the works and gradually discovered how things really were. When he arrived he was determined that nobody was going to give him a shabby deal and rather got off on the wrong foot. Grandfather had left a load of dynamite in the family cellar.

In fact Eric turned out to be a competent administrator and I was soon able to put him in charge of the production of pewter and electroplate. In those early years there was no shortage of orders. We got on together quite well but underneath there was always his ingrained feeling that he had to fight for a fair crack of the whip, that his talents were not fully appreciated and mine were perhaps over-valued.

We worked together to see what we could make of the electroplate and pewter business. I decided to have another look at Father's invention of 'machine engraving'. Decoration was becoming more acceptable in post-war design so I decided to have a go at making electro-formed dies to put 'engraved' designs on spun teasets. By that time the technique of electro-depositing iron from a hot solution of ferrous chloride was well established. Eric and I successfully made dies to produce 'engraved' patterns that were indistinguishable from the real thing.

We split off Land Pyrometers

Both the old business and the new were doing well. I decided that we would split them into separate companies and in 1950 we formed Land Pyrometers Ltd. I gave serious thought to splitting the business between the two sides of the family, giving Eric and Harold the old family business and keeping the new Land Pyrometers for Father and myself. But Eric was young and inexperienced and the practical and financial difficulties looked too formidable. The chance went by.

Learning to be engineers - and accountants

When we had established our resale business we were soon drawn into manufacturing. Our customers needed thermocouples complete with sheaths and terminal heads. We engaged a welder to close the ends of the metal sheaths and we set to work to design a

THE FOUNDING OF LAND PYROMETERS 47

thermocouple head and other accessories for thermocouples.

Roy Marsh found an engineer who had some old machine tools on which he could machine the flanges, elbows and collars that we needed. He was also prepared to machine the graphite sleeves that we used on our liquid steel thermocouples. By 1950 we were almost his only customer and I suggested to him that it would be wise for him to come and work for us. We bought his old lathes and drilling machines and installed them in the basement of the factory among the spinning lathes and drop-stamps belonging to the pewter business. Thus we engaged Fred Nickols, his young assistant Tony Dickinson and the lads who operated the machines.

We were accustomed to manufacturing but all our work in the pewter business was hand craftsmanship. Engineering was a whole new world in which we had no experience at all. Unfortunately we soon found that Fred Nickols was really an electrician and we hadn't a real engineer on the place. When we came to make anything more complicated than a machined casting we were soon out of our depth and in real trouble.

Eric gradually got the problems sorted out. He introduced parts lists and part numbers and then he had the good fortune to recruit a real engineer. Bill Longley came to us as a capstan lathe operator but he had been in charge of a machine shop during the war. Sadly, we decided that Fred Nickols would have to go. What happened then is vividly described by Tony Dickinson, who had moved up to the stores by this time and who had talent for writing that nobody had guessed until much later. This is an extract from an account of our early days that he wrote for me.

> 'One Monday morning Jim Wortley came up from the machine shop and said, in his broad Sheffield accent, "Owd Nicko's got the bullet". "Tha wot?" said I, not taking in what had been said. "Owd Nick's got the push" repeated Jim. "I'll go downstairs and wish him goodbye", I said. "Too late" said Jim, "he left Friday night". So the man I had worked for all my working life passed out of my life without even a chance to say so long and I never saw him again. Bill Longley was put in charge and, after the mutterings about "that rotten lot upstairs" had died away it became apparent that "they" knew what they were doing. Bill brought a new discipline into the production line, production runs went through and, what's more, the parts were interchangeable'.

The management course that I had attended before the war taught me how to prepare management accounts. Within a few years I was preparing not only sales analyses every month but also monthly balance sheets and profit and loss accounts. So we had a good control of the financial situation from the beginning.

The valuation of the inventory is always a problem. In our little business I found a very simple solution. Most of our sales were of items that we bought on a re-sale discount.

I grouped our purchases according to their resale discount. We bought all refractories on a 25% resale discount, and each other group was selected to keep all items of equal discount in one category. At the month end we took the opening stock, added the purchases and subtracted the sales at their cost prices. When we came to manufacture instruments I adopted the convention that the cost of a finished article was half the selling price. Work in progress was simply valued at the cost of the component parts. It was simple and perfectly adequate.

Now that we had got Land Pyrometers up and running I could set about another task that was more difficult but more interesting to me and ultimately became much more important. I started the business that became Land Infrared. For more than 20 years we kept the two businesses running together using the same sales force and the same production organization. In the early days the infrared business was just too small to stand on its own; even after 20 years it was only one quarter the size of Land Pyrometers. Without this close support from the thermocouple business we could never have built Land Infrared. Yet the two businesses were so very different and distinct that I have decided to tell the story of Land Infrared in a separate chapter; but it should be remembered how closely they were entwined for all those early years.

Designing equipment that is high class and 'user-friendly'

During these first few years we were learning a great deal and learning fast. We established ourselves as suppliers of thermocouples and spares for the steel industry and we set up accounting procedures. We began to learn about engineering. I was determined that we would be no second-rate business. We would set the highest standards in design, accuracy and service.

I had the great advantage of having spent several years doing the job that our customers did - keeping the pyrometers in a steelworks in good working order. I decided that we would make equipment that was designed to be easy for them to use and service. The thermocouple head is a good example. We designed one that was easy to fit to the thick thermocouple wires into, that was free from the errors that can arise if the two terminals are at different temperatures. We also provided a tapered hole for the wires of the compensating cable to facilitate their entry into the terminal block. Loose screws were made captive so that they did not disappear down cracks and holes in the shop floor at the wrong moment. The design, shown in Fig. 3.2, remained essentially unchanged for 35 years and was then copied by a competitor!

We sold the special compensating cable that must be used to connect a thermocouple to the meter that indicates or records the temperature. I knew from experience that some instrument companies were careless about the quality of their cable. We took the greatest care to avoid the errors that can occur if the special wires used in the cable do not have

THE FOUNDING OF LAND PYROMETERS

exactly the same thermoelectric characteristics as the wires of the thermocouple. Instrument companies bought their cable from cable manufacturers, usually leaving the wire specification in the manufacturer's hands. That was not good enough for us. We had wire specially made for us to our specifications, tested it carefully and sent it off to be made into cable. We then checked the cable to make sure that the makers had used our wire, not their own!

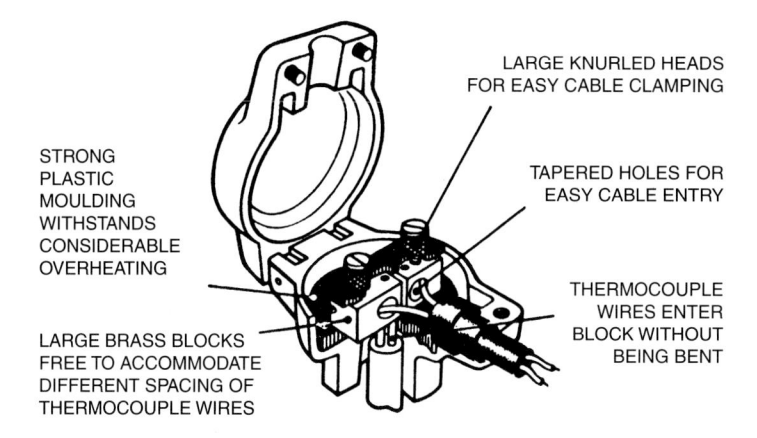

Fig. 3.2 The thermocouple head designed to be efficient and easy to use.

Our competitors, the Amalgams Company, gave excellent service to their customers. If a customer in South Wales needed something in a hurry, Bill Platts would put it in his car and drive down to South Wales straight away - and there were no motorways in those days! So we quickly learned to do the same. Good service was also encouraged by our practice of recruiting our salesmen largely from the ranks of our customers. A man who has experienced the desperate need for good service in an emergency is most likely to respond willingly when it is required of him.

Finance for the growing business

When a business grows as rapidly as ours did it needs an increasing amount of finance. We were unable in the early years to retain much of our profit in the business because we had to support the older generation of the Land family. They were drawing salaries but not, of course, contributing much to the activity of the business. In the first three post-war years the older generation received salaries which totalled £11,681, which represented about 7% of the sales in those years. So there was not much left to plough back.

My slogan at the time was that we needed to "mobilise the resources of the business", meaning borrow from the bank what we needed to finance our growth. We could not support the older generation without a business of a more substantial size. The combined sales of our two companies grew to £110,000 in the year 1951/2 and the overdraft grew to £12,685 at 31 March 1952. Father was not too happy about that.

The electroplate and pewter business is sold

Our growing business was also running out of space with two businesses squeezed into one factory. In the basement the lathes and drilling machines belonging to Land Pyrometers were all mixed up with the spinning lathes and drop-stamps of T. Land and Son. Father and I talked over our problems and we decided that we could now safely depend on Land Pyrometers which had grown to be three quarters of the whole enterprise and was growing fast. It would release capital and give us more space if we disposed of our pewter business. So we set out to visit other pewter manufacturers in Sheffield to seek a buyer for T. Land and Son Ltd. We were fortunate to make a successful deal with E.H. Parkin and Co of Scotland St. who bought all the stock and equipment as well as the trade-mark CIVIC.

We retained T. Land and Son Ltd as a separate company that owned the factory. Father sold the business that had been his life's work without any hesitation or complaint, he was convinced it was the right decision. He had spent long years expending his great talents in a dying industry and I feel sure that he was glad to be in a new business with encouraging prospects. We had succeeded in the difficult task of switching the family business out of the electroplate trade, that had served the family well for a hundred years, into a new industry where we would be more successful than we had ever been. It was quite an achievement.

In the year 1951-2 our sales had topped £80,000 and during the next four years Roy Marsh rapidly increased our share of the market until in the year 1955-6 our sales reached £200,000. This was a great achievement, but it posed a question: where do we go from here? We had run out of capital and we had filled the factory.

Where do we go from here?

By this time I was 42 and watching the best part of my life going by. Ten years before, I had set out with a clear objective: I would first build a simple business like the Amalgams Company and on that firm base I would build an instrument business. I had achieved the first part, but I had no idea how I was going to achieve the second part. What I really needed to do was to sit back for a while, reduce our overhead expenses, get the business profitable and put a bit of money in the bank. But I was in too much of a hurry and it didn't look as simple as that at the time. I knew that we were certainly going to need more factory space, so I set out to find some land to build a new factory. Audrey and I went all over Sheffield and its surroundings looking for a suitable site. To our dismay we could find nothing suitable in Sheffield. The best that we could come up with was 3˘ acres of good flat ground in Dronfield. The idea of moving out to Dronfield was a little daunting but there was no realistic alternative. The land would cost £5,408; unfortunately we did not have the money.

I had begun to read the books of Peter Drucker on business management and I knew that I should ask 'what is our business?' and also 'what should our business be?' I could answer the first question, the second one was much more difficult. At that time our business was easily defined. We were suppliers of thermocouples and spares to the pyrometry departments of British steel works and glass works. We also made radiation thermometers, but in 1956 the sales were quite insignificant. This was more a hobby than a business. I thought that we should set out to be a "real" instrument company, making indicators, recorders, controllers, not just thermocouples. This judgement was totally wrong and led us to make many mistakes.

The first mistake was the London Office. Roy Marsh thought that there would be plenty of business in the South of England if we had a man down in London to search it out. So in 1956 we established an office at 227 Holland Park Avenue. Fritz Steghart's instrument business had run into trouble and his sales manager Ian Gordon was looking for a job. We knew him and liked him so we put him in charge of the London Office. It seemed to me to be a good idea for us to develop a wider-based sales organization ready for the day when we would start making instruments. Unfortunately the London office increased our costs and made our business more complicated to run, but brought in very little extra business.

We also spent a lot of time developing a millivoltmeter. We used a portable temperature indicator in conjunction with our surface pyrometer. We bought it from the Cambridge Instrument Company and it was a good meter. I thought a portable meter would be a good place to start in my ambition to become a real instrument company. We would first develop a portable indicator and then we could move on to produce panel-mounted meters, recorders and controllers.

Our indicator was to be no ordinary instrument. The problem with galvanometer indicators, and particularly with portable ones, is that the finely pointed steel pivots, that carry the coil and the pointer and move in jewels, like a watch movement, are readily damaged. When this happens the meter ceases to move freely and it is necessary to tap it to get a correct reading. We decided to solve this problem and we did. We made a movement mounted on three large coil springs that isolated it from shock. We could roll it down a flight of stone stairs and pick it up quite undamaged. We went to a London designer who produced an attractive and unusual case for it. In due course it went into production and was much admired.

All this was doing nothing to address our real problems, which began to get worse instead of better during 1957. Having been reading Peter Drucker, I decided to call a meeting of managers and sales people to discuss "the past achievements, the present problems and the future plans of the company." It was held in October 1957 at the Rising Sun Hotel, Bamford, and was a successful event which we decided to repeat the next year. But we did not get down to the bed-rock problems of the business.

It was about this time that we had the first offer from another company to buy Lands. It came from the Cambridge Instrument Company, a business with a distinguished history, founded by Erasmus Darwin, son of the great Charles Darwin. At first I wondered whether this would be a short cut to my dream of running an instrument company, but I found that they had no idea what they would do with Lands if they bought us. I had to get back to answering my own questions.

We get financial investment from ICFC

There were some things that we could get on with. First we decided to simplify the structure of the business by putting all the assets of T. Land and Son Ltd (which owned the factory) and Land Pyrometers Ltd together into a new company. We then put both companies into voluntary liquidation and changed the name of the new company to Land Pyrometers Ltd. That is how it comes about that Land Pyrometers Ltd appears to have been started in 1956 when in fact it was established in 1950.

Next I decided that I must tackle the problem of finance. On the advice of the Bank I made a preliminary visit to the Industrial and Commercial Finance Corporation (ICFC) which had been set up by the Bank of England and the clearing banks to serve small companies such as ours which were too small to seek a public issue. On 23 January 1957 we held a director's meeting to discuss the question of finance. There was a strong clash of opinions in which my father was opposed to my plans. The minutes of the meeting record the occasion quite vividly.

> 'Discussions took place regarding the advisability of seeking the investment of outside capital in the business for working capital and to finance the building of a new factory. Mr. F.W. Land and Mr. G.R. Marsh were of the opinion that this should be delayed and that we should drastically reduce the rapid rate of growth of the business to enable the present financial position to be improved. Ways and means should be explored of increasing the profitability of the business. In this way we would be able to go much further towards financing the expansion of the business ourselves without the investment of outside capital.
>
> 'However the other three directors were of the opinion that our need for extra working capital was immediate and that this could only be met by

seeking this investment of outside capital. Furthermore the business could only be put on a sound financial footing by virtually coming to a standstill for several years. They felt that it would be a mistaken policy to strangle the growth of a flourishing business. The reasons for the low profits so far this year were apparent and higher profits could be expected next year. Furthermore we could never make sufficient profit to finance the rapid growth of the business. Mr. F.W. Land and Mr. G.R. Marsh expressed their willingness to support our Managing Director in the policy which he wished to pursue although they felt it was a mistaken one.

'It was proposed by Mr. T. Land and seconded by Mr. E.H. Land and carried unanimously that: Mr. T. Land should approach the Industrial and Commercial Finance Corporation Ltd again and ask them to invest £15,000 in the business for working capital and £5,000 to enable the land at Dronfield to be purchased immediately; and a further £15,000 during 1958 or 1959 to help finance the building of the factory.'

I took John Grosse from our accountants with me to the ICFC office in Leeds where we had discussions with a tall, courteous and impressive young man called Alan Martin. I think that Alan was intrigued by our presentation with graphs on semi-logarithmic graph paper. We got on very well together - indeed we appeared together a few years later on a BBC television program on finance for small businesscs. It was finally decided that ICFC would take a small share-holding in Land Pyrometers and would provide a £20,000 debenture for working capital and to finance future growth. This injection of capital required minor changes in the capital structure of the company which were carried out in July 1957. At that time Roy Barber, who had been made a director in May of that year, acquired his first 700 shares. With the ICFC money in the bank we were able to buy the land at Dronfield, but not yet to build the new factory.

My father's hesitation was perfectly understandable. There had been no previous recourse to financial institutions to provide extra working capital for the growing family business. Instead the family had brought in friends as working partners, notably my mother's uncle Walter Oxley. ICFC was something new and quite different, created specially to meet the needs of firms such as ours. We have always found them helpful and unobtrusive, a reassuring presence in the background, available in case of need or opportunity.

A dramatic change of policy

Looking back to the late 1950s it is clear that in the previous decade we had succeeded in acquiring a fair share of the market that the Amalgams Company had previously had to themselves. By about 1957, although we did not know it, we had got nearly all that was coming our way - just at the time that we ran out of money. Our sales of thermocouples and spares remained at a very similar level for a further 20 years and did so with a minimum of selling cost. In 1958 the British steel industry met its first recession since the war and our sales fell by 20%; as a result our profits disappeared. I sat at my desk and calculated the speed at which our working capital would disappear if I continued with our existing policies.

As the year 1958 progressed things went from bad to worse and I realized that I had to change my priorities. I had concentrated mainly on growth. Now I had to accept the business that I had and make it profitable. I worked out that I needed to cut our costs by at least £10,000 a year. This was a lot of money in those days. It would not come from a few savings here and there, we had to save the cost of some big salaries, I needed a new and simpler management structure.

At such a moment it is wise to look for a model to follow and I had one close at hand. The Amalgams Company had been on the job for nearly 50 years and their organization was a streamlined machine that worked beautifully. I found out what I could about their simple organization and I soon saw how we could make the savings that we needed. I had come round to the advice that my father had given at the Board meeting whose minutes I have quoted.

Although Roy Marsh had supported Father and his words of wisdom he did not find it easy to accept the practical consequences when it was seen that much of the cost-cutting would fall on the Sales Department. We needed more sales, so surely we needed more salesmen, not fewer! Ironically, he had bought a copy of the book 'Parkinson's Law' which we both enjoyed. Its simple conclusion was that there is no relation between the size of a task and the number of people needed to carry it out; work expands to fill the time available. This is exactly what had happened to us but Roy was unable to see it at the time.

Doing the unthinkable

Over many anxious days and sleepless nights I reviewed every possible course of action. In the end I found that I had to be prepared to think the unthinkable and to ask myself what would happen if Roy Marsh were to go. It was a deeply painful thought, disloyal to an old friend and a good colleague who had done more than anyone to build the business.

It also looked dangerous. What would be the impact on the salesmen, on the customers, even on suppliers who were his friends? Would the business flounder without Roy's dynamic drive? Who would look after the export market? I got very little encouragement for the idea from Father or from Audrey, but Eric, whose relations with Roy had never been cordial, was less averse to the idea. He had always resented Roy's position as

No. 2 to me. In the end I was sufficiently distressed by Roy's intransigence to take the painful decision; he would have to go if we were to become the healthy and profitable business that we so desperately needed to be. Against the advice of my father and the misgivings of Audrey I steeled myself and went ahead.

Roy was dumbfounded and incredulous and I did not blame him. He was given a year's salary for loss of office. To my intense relief he walked straight into a good job where he stayed until he retired. We closed the London office; Ian Gordon was not at all surprised and he immediately got a good job with the Cambridge Instrument Company.

We had tried to cost all of our many special thermocouples and other instruments and the expense was quite ridiculous. We reduced the cost department to one girl and the sales department to two outside salesmen and one inside. I myself took over responsibility for sales. All telephone enquiries for stock items were routed directly to the stores where they knew all the answers. I had a daily meeting at 9.00 a.m. to look at the mail and discuss any outstanding problems. Any salesman who was in the office joined me and Eric and Roy Barber and gave us their reports on their recent activities.

The effect of all these dismissals was unsettling and there were those who thought that we were going down the drain. We soon lost both our outside salesmen and we had to recruit a new sales force in a hurry. Jack Glew, who had worked for me as a boy at Jessops, had joined our little research and development team in 1958. We persuaded him to try his hand at selling which he did very successfully. We were lucky also to pick up Graham Torr who had been a salesman for Leeds and Northrup. The two of them made a much better team than we had had before.

It had been a traumatic experience for everyone and there were times early in 1959 when I wondered if everything that I had worked for was going to fall to pieces. In the event everyone worked together marvellously and we established a much better organization. Eric and I began a period of 20 years during which we worked together to build our business. Our financial position was rapidly transformed, helped by the recovery of the steel industry and by the growth in sales of radiation thermometers which began, at last, to make a significant contribution to sales and profits. Whereas the profit in 1958/9 was not much more than £4,000, the year 1959/60 produced a profit of more than £25,000. An overdraft of nearly £15,000 was paid off and we finished the year with £19,000 in the bank.

Celebration

In the spring of 1960 the business was doing so well after its great shake-up that I decided that we needed to celebrate. Grandfather had, rather arbitrarily, chosen 1860 as the date of the foundation of the business - 'Established 1860'. So I decided that we would celebrate our centenary and do it in style. In the spring of 1960 we chartered two Dakotas to fly us from Derby airport to Holland. Then coaches took us on a tour of the bulb-fields which were ablaze with colour. We visited Scheveningen and Rotterdam, taking in lunch and dinner on the way. Fig. 3.3 shows one of the Dakota ready for take-off and Fig. 3.4 shows one of the party taking a rest. Few of our people had ever been on an aeroplane and it was all a tremendous thrill and a great success. Two years earlier the wonderful Manchester United football club had been nearly destroyed in the air crash at Munich. We took care who flew together in our two planes in case one of ours should crash.

Fig. 3.3
One of the Dakotas ready for take-off.

Fig. 3.4
Brenda Staniforth with the bulb fields in the background.

I was aware that we had come through this testing time successfully only because everybody had responded so enthusiastically to the challenge. I wanted to share some of the fruits of our success with everyone who had helped to make it possible. So at the end of 1959 we declared a special Christmas bonus of 2°% of their year's earnings for all our employees. It was so well received that we decided to make it an annual event. In this way we began our policy of profit-sharing that has been an important part of our business ever since. It began as a simple thank-you and that is the way that I think that it should be seen.

THE FOUNDING OF LAND PYROMETERS 57

Building a factory at Dronfield

Each year we now made a profit of £30,000 to £40,000. We paid off some of our loans and in 1962, with £40,000 in the bank, we decided that we could afford to build the new factory on our land at Dronfield. We engaged Husband and Company, (who had recently designed the Jodrell Bank radio telescope) to design us a factory; this design was sent out to tender to 6 or 8 builders. We had expected to have to spend about £65,000 but when we opened the tenders they were all between £85,000 and £105,000 - far more than we could afford.

However we heard of a firm in Leeds who offered a package deal of design and construction and we went to see them. Their proposals were much more reasonable in price, so we went back to Husbands and showed them what we could get elsewhere. There was a great flurry of activity. Husbands knew that Finnegans were on the verge of becoming a public company and wanted plenty of contracts in hand to impress the City. So we went through the plans and cut out all the frills and unnecessary over-specification and let Finnegans re-quote. On 6th December 1962 the board resolved "to accept the tender submitted by Messrs. J.F. Finnegan and Co. (Sheffield) Ltd for the sum of sixty-seven thousand, five hundred and fifteen pounds eight shillings and one penny". We sold the Queens Road factory to Sheffield Corporation for £16,000 and on 16th December, 1963 we moved into the new factory at Dronfield. This first stage of the Dronfield factory is illustrated in Fig. 3.5. The picture shows only the office block. The large factory bay behind the offices, which housed the machine shop and the assembly areas, can just be glimpsed on the left-hand side of the picture. The bay was demolished in 1995.

Fig. 3.5 Our new factory at Dronfield, January 1964

The growth of the sales of Land Pyrometers while we were at Queens Road is shown by the graph (Fig. 3.6) in which the upper curve represents the sales of thermocouples and spares. The big dip in the sales of thermocouples in 1958 caused us to reorganize the business. The subsequent steep rise in sales from 1960 and the arrival of significant sales of radiation pyrometers gave us the very profitable period that financed the building of the first stage of the Dronfield factory.

The lower curve in the bottom right-hand corner represents the birth of Lands as it is today. The sudden rise from zero in 1959 simply represents the fact that before 1960 the sales of infrared thermometers were too small to be worth recording separately. By the time that we moved to Dronfield it was beginning to dawn on me that the instrument company that I had dreamt of building, and was beginning to despair of in 1957, was starting to take shape. It was not going to be a 'proper instrument company' making indicators, recorders and controllers like Cambridge or Kents or Honeywell. It was going to be something new that had hardly been thought of at that time, a specialist 'niche' company making a special type of instrument and selling to a world market.

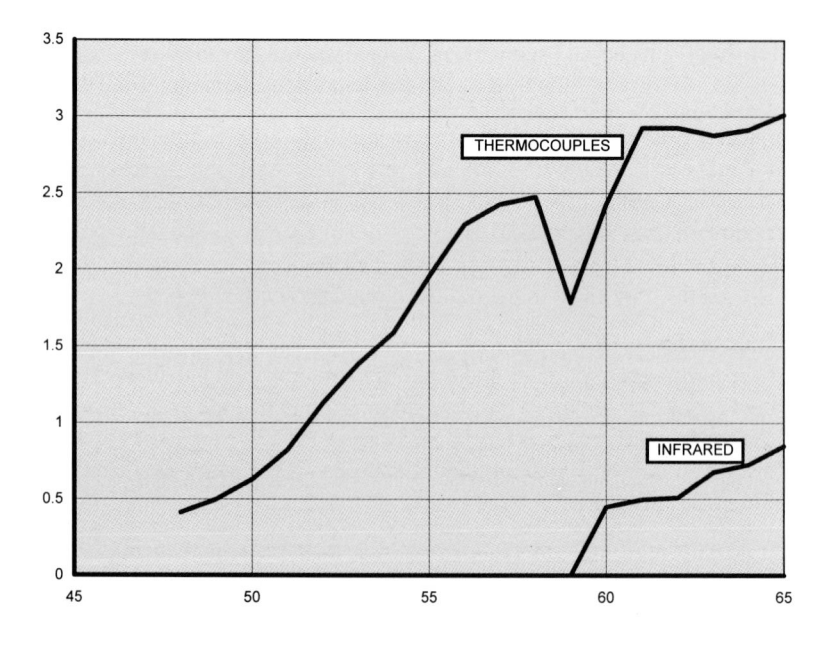

Fig. 3.6 The growth of sales of Land Pyrometers at Queens Road

CHAPTER 4
THE ELECTRONITE CONNECTION
1964 to 1989

Disposable liquid steel thermocouples

Measurements in liquid steel had always been central to the business of Land Pyrometers. The silica tubes, used to protect the platinum rhodium thermocouple, and discarded after every measurement, were our largest selling line. The technique invented in England was taken up by American steelworks after the war. By about 1960, they had decided that it was time to redesign the thermocouples to make them easier to maintain and to make their accuracy more precise.

The redesign required the co-operation of an instrument company (Leeds & Northrup) and a major steelworks. This time the design was in the hands of professional engineers with an intimate knowledge of American steelworks practice. The world had also moved on. New components were available such as metal sheathed mineral insulated thermocouple extension cable that would withstand red-hot temperatures. The development of the design can be followed from successive Leeds and Northrup patents and from evidence given in a patent infringement trial.

The British design used a carbon end-block to protect the hot end of the thermocouple arm from the corrosive slag and the liquid steel in which it was immersed. But lying around an American steel melting furnace were lengths of thick cardboard tube. To open up the tap hole and let the molten steel run out of the ladle a blast of pure oxygen was passed down a long steel lance into the tap-hole. The cardboard tubes were used to protect the oxygen lance from the liquid steel as it gushed out. The same cheap cardboard tubes were used for protection in the new design of the thermocouple.

They decided to throw away after each immersion not only the silica protection tube but also the platinum thermocouple and the cardboard tube. They reduced the diameter of the platinum thermocouple to only a few thousandth of an inch and they protected it, not with a closed ended sheath, but with a U-tube of silica open at both ends. A neat little concentric connector joined the thermocouple to the mineral insulated extension lead. It was a brilliant design.

The principal patents of the new design were held by Leeds and Northrup, so when I heard of the development I went to Leeds and Northrup's British subsidiary and enquired whether we might manufacture the thermocouple under licence. I met with a firm refusal. The Amalgams Company had negotiated the right to sell the Honeywell version of the thermocouple and we were left out in the cold.

A visit from Henk Kleyn

But we struck lucky. One day in 1963 we had a visit from a Dutchman called Henk Kleyn who was in charge of the European subsidiary of an American company called ElectroNite Engineering. They were manufacturing a different design of disposable thermocouple and Henk offered us the right to distribute it in Britain. I arranged for him to give us a demonstration at the Vickers Works of the English Steel Corporation and I was very favourably impressed.

Henk had brought a long thermocouple arm consisting of a length of mild steel tube with a cable connection at one end and a 2 ft length of smaller diameter steel tube at the other. Over this smaller diameter section he slid the disposable unit that looked like a 2ft length of cardboard tube with a small steel cap protruding from the closed end (Fig. 4.1). A cable was connected from the thermocouple arm to the temperature recorder and the furnaceman immersed the cardboard tube in the liquid steel through the opened furnace door. Within 10 seconds we had a good trace on the recorder and the thermocouple was withdrawn and laid on the stage. The charred cardboard tube was pulled off and handed to me. Although the exposed part of the thermocouple arm had become red-hot, the cardboard had rapidly cooled and had provided excellent thermal protection for the steel tube that it had covered.

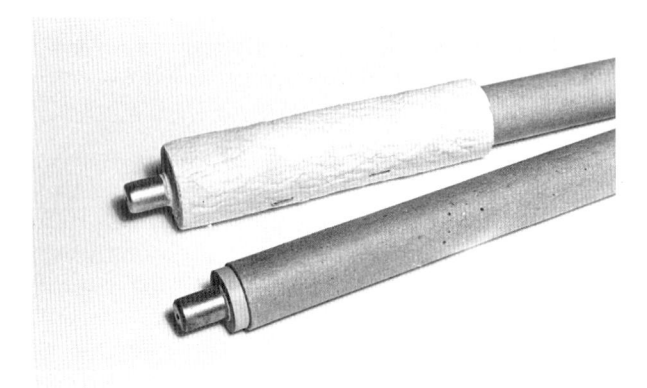

Fig. 4.1 The ElectroNite disposable thermocouple and a modification (above) used in foundries. The steel cap protects the silica U-tube from the slag

This was quite obviously a great advance on the original designs that we were using in Britain. My next question was whether the steel companies would pay the much higher price that was involved. The high labour cost in American steelworks allowed the cost of the new units to be paid for by the lower cost of maintenance. But in Britain it was not certain that the savings would be sufficient.

The patent litigation in America

Then there was the question of the patent. Most of the original work on the thermocouple had been done by Leeds and Northrup and they had a formidable array of patents. A family called Littman had a business in Philadelphia called ElectroNite where they made graphite components, including graphite parts for liquid steel thermocouples. When they heard what was going on they had decided that they too would be in the business of disposable thermocouples and the son of the family, Larry Littman, had set up a company that they called ElectroNite Engineering for this purpose. They had engaged a brilliant young engineer who had designed for them a thermocouple that was at least as good as the Leeds and Northrup unit and cheaper to make. They had taken out patents on this design and Leeds and Northrup had challenged them in the American courts. The litigation went on for several years. I insisted that we must be able to manufacture the thermocouple in England and that we must wait to see the outcome of the patent litigation before we became involved.

We sell more shares to ICFC to meet family death duties

While we were waiting for the litigation to be settled we decided that we needed to think again about the family finances. The older generation were in their eighties; my mother had died in 1963 at the age of 83, my aunt was 85 and my father was 89. There would be death duties to pay on their estates; estates whose value was largely locked up in the business. We discussed the situation with ICFC and it was agreed that they would buy some of the family shares to bring their holding up to about 43%. The family retained 51% and Roy Barber had the remainder. The reorganization was carried out on 31st March, 1965. My aunt died in 1964 and my father in December 1965, a few days before his 91st birthday. I had great respect and affection for him and I missed him more than I had believed possible. But life went on.

We start to manufacture Dipstiks

When the litigation between ElectroNite and Leeds and Northrup was clearly seen to be moving in favour of ElectroNite we began to set up manufacturing facilities. We built a special workshop at the far end of No.1 bay of the Dronfield factory, installed spot-welding machines that we bought through ElectroNite and began to learn to make disposable thermocouples. We also began to think of a name for them; Graham Torr eventually came up with the name Dipstik which we liked and adopted.

When we started to test the thermocouples in the steelworks we were disappointed because we did not always get good traces on the recorder. We spent many months trying to find what was wrong and Eric and I went to America to discuss our problems with ElectroNite. They were not particularly helpful and maintained that they had no such problems; but we discovered that they had quite a lot of problems and it turned out that they were better at selling than at manufacturing. The quality control at their American plant left a lot to be desired in those days.

Once we were satisfied that we had solved the manufacturing problems we set about reorganizing our sales department. Fred Campbell was made Sales Manager and became a director in July 1966. We increased the sales force and put them temporarily on commission to increase their enthusiasm for this important new product.

I decided that we would not sell at a price lower than Leeds and Northrup but would rely on our superior quality and excellent service. This suited Leeds and Northrup very well. They did not want a price war any more than we did and they were established in the market. Our advantage of a lower cost product was offset by the fact that we had to pay 5% royalty to ElectroNite and also 5% to Leeds and Northrup.

Dipstiks soon double our thermocouple sales

In the year ending 31 March 1967 our Dipstik sales were £43k, the next year £138k (equal to all other thermocouples), then £192k, £260k and in 1970/71 £300k. In four years we had become the major supplier of disposable thermocouples in the U.K. and the American management of Leeds and Northrup were not amused. They sent a dynamic salesman over to the U.K. to rectify the situation.

He had no interest in our tacit understanding about prices. He brought a new, cut-price Leeds and Northrup thermocouple that he believed would sweep the board. The ElectroNite design used smaller diameter cardboard tubes than the original L & N model. The new L & N unit was designed with the same smaller diameter tubes. Unfortunately they had always maintained that their units were superior to ours because they used larger tubes and their remaining customers were those who accepted this to be true! As L & N reduced their prices we reduced ours (very slowly) and because of our good quality and service we lost few important customers. The steel industry benefitted, we lost profit margin, but L & N finished up selling about the same number of thermocouples at much reduced prices. The American super-salesman went home.

Bill Longley and Tony Duncan become directors of Land Pyrometers

Until 1968 we had left it to our accountants to prepare our accounts and I had prepared our quarterly management accounts myself. ICFC sent one of their management consultants called Peter Smith to spend a few days with us and we decided that we were large enough to benefit from employing an accountant of our own. We advertised for an accountant and had quite a number of applicants. Peter Smith, who was himself an

THE ELECTRONITE CONNECTION 63

accountant, offered to interview the candidates while Eric and I sat in and listened to an impressive display of interviewing technique. Despite the brilliant technique we failed to find a suitable candidate. However a further candidate turned up on the Saturday morning after Peter Smith had gone home. He seemed to be a sensible down-to-earth sort of fellow who might just suit us, so we engaged him. His name was Tony Duncan. He soon became Company Secretary and then, in 1972, a Director of the Company. Even without Peter Smith we had done rather well.

We also added another member to the Board. All manufacturing had always been part of Eric's responsibility and he had come to depend increasingly on Bill Longley. The accounts department also came under Eric's wing, so Tony was responsible to Eric for his day to day activities. This fitted in well with my philosophy of doing only those things that other people could not do equally well. But as a director, he was responsible to me as Chairman and Managing Director, so I could talk to him about the management accounts which were my ultimate responsibility. Eric suggested that it would be logical for Bill Longley to be a director as well and I was happy to agree. So in 1974 Bill, who had joined us as a capstan lathe operator, became a member of the Board.

Fig. 4.2 The Directors of Land Pyrometers in 1974.
Standing: Bill Longley, Fred Campbell, Tony Duncan, Roy Barber.
Seated: Eric Land, Tom Land, Harold Land (Eric's father).

The Sampla and the Leigh Oxygen Probe

In 1969 we began work on another disposable product for liquid steel. Steelmakers had adopted spectroscopic methods of chemical analysis for the new rapid oxygen steel-melting processes and they needed new rapid methods of taking samples of liquid steel that could be quickly quenched and sent to the laboratory. The British Steel Corporation brought us their design of sampling probe which we began to manufacture in 1970. With a flash of originality we named it 'the Sampla' and it was followed by a range of similar sampling probes for different applications. They produced substantial sales but less profit than we would have liked.

A third important disposable product now appeared. We had heard that work was going on to produce an electro-chemical cell that would measure the oxygen content of liquid steel. This is one of the key measurements in steel making. Oxygen must be introduced into liquid iron to remove the excess carbon as carbon dioxide. The process must then be stopped at the right moment by adding aluminium or other deoxidizing agents to the steel. Nowadays this is done in the ladle. An accurate knowledge of the oxygen content of the liquid metal allows the addition to be calculated accurately and economically.

News came to us from the BISRA laboratories in Sheffield that the Canadian National Research Council had produced a successful oxygen probe which was being manufactured in Ottawa by Leigh Instruments. We were convinced that oxygen probes would have a big future so I arranged to go to Ottawa to have a look at the new probes. I saw a demonstration in a small arc furnace and saw several measurements made. Again there was a cardboard tube with the measuring unit mounted on the end, but this time it was a small zirconia cap with a platinum electrode attached to it. As the oxygen ions from the liquid steel diffused through the zirconia, they produced a small electric current that was determined by the oxygen content of the steel. The results were impressive and I decided to enter into negotiations for us to import the Leigh oxygen probe to sell in the U.K. This would give us a full range of disposable products - Dipstiks, Samplas and oxygen probes, all with the same basic construction of a measuring or sampling unit mounted at the end of a cardboard tube.

In 1969 Fred Campbell had been keen to try to extend sales of the thermocouple side of the business into Europe. The new range of sampling devices that we were developing looked promising for the European market. So in January 1970 we decided to investigate the possibility of forming a European company. When the oxygen probe arrived on the scene the idea of a European company made a great deal more sense. We found that Leigh were already negotiating with a distributor in Europe but I managed to persuade them to let us have a go in Europe as well as in the U.K. At the back of my mind I always had the anxiety that we were too much dependent on ElectroNite and that our liquid steel business was far too much confined to the small British market.

Land Europe, a failure

We decided to base our business in Belgium and I went to Brussels to find someone to take charge of our European operation. It turned out to be more difficult to find a good man than I had imagined. We went to an agency where our requirements were put in the hands of an energetic man called Edgard Wauters who was about 60 years old and had been manager of a foundry that had been closed down. When we failed to find anybody suitable Edgard said to me "I would like to be a candidate". Liking the man, and in spite of his age, I decided to take him on. He proved to be wonderfully energetic and was an excellent choice. He spoke English, French, German and Flemish fluently and had a sound basis of business experience. So in July 1970 I went again to Belgium and put the formation of Land Europe S.A. in the hands of the Brussels office of Peat Marwick Mitchell. Edgard Wauters found an excellent little warehouse and office and recruited an assistant. By the end of 1970 we were in business in Europe.

After arriving at Dronfield we had recruited several excellent people, among them David Coe, who had taken a degree in physics at Oxford and had worked at Lands during the vacations. Dave worked with Edgard to get a foothold in the European steel industry. It was an uphill struggle which was made much more difficult when we began to have serious problems with the Leigh oxygen probe. Leigh were specialists in avionics and were not really at home with steelworks instruments, much less with the considerable problems of electrochemistry at very high temperatures.

But there was more to it than the indifferent quality of the probes. We were 10 years too soon for the market and we found it most difficult to raise any enthusiasm for oxygen measurement in the British Steel industry (although today there is a great demand for it). We also found local competition with inexpensive and well designed samplers coming into the European market, so our progress was slow. Land Europe lost £5,000 in the 3 months to 31 March 1971. Despite our valiant efforts our European venture never got off the ground and early in 1973 we reluctantly withdrew. You don't win them all.

The profitable seventies

The nineteen seventies saw Britain getting into ever deeper economic trouble with the trades unions wielding far too much power for the good of the nation. The long period of full employment after the war was becoming increasingly difficult to sustain. The governments, with the best of intentions, were following policies aiming to sustain employment but succeeding instead in stimulating inflation. Nevertheless steel production grew and Land Pyrometers prospered. Between 1972 and 1979 the sales of dipstiks in real terms increased by two thirds to £2 million of 1987 money and Samplas grew from nothing to £1 million (1987).

As the Government wrestled with inflation, they introduced prices and incomes controls which might have clipped the wings of our profitability. But still we managed to turn the price controls to our advantage to keep profit margins high; the customer could not easily complain about prices that were sanctioned by the Government! So in the year to 31st March 1979 we made a profit of £684k on sales of £4.64 million.

Adjusting for inflation

This profit was calculated after making adjustment for inflation. As inflation slipped out of the control of successive governments we realized that conventional historic cost accounting practices seriously overstated the real profits of a business. A proposal for dealing with this situation was put forward by the accountancy profession but it got bogged down with academic quibbles and political pressure and was never adopted. We decided that the matter was too serious for us to wait for a decision and adopted our own inflation accounting practice for our management accounts. We still use the system, which saved us from the complacency that led so many British manufacturing companies into trouble during that period. We set tough but realistic targets and achieved them throughout that time.

As inflation got worse and worse we had to increase wages and salaries to compensate for the ever increasing cost of living. I thought about the anxiety that everyone was facing as prices rose and rose. I decided that we were dishonest if we pretended that we were generously increasing wages and salaries. Common honesty demanded that all remuneration should be automatically adjusted every year to maintain its purchasing power. We should then make other adjustments as a separate exercise. To emphasise the separation of the two adjustments they were made at different times of the year. All salaries are still linked to the cost of living index as a matter of common honesty.

I tend to look back on the sixties and seventies as halcyon years when business came easily and profits were good. Of course it was by no means as simple as it may appear in retrospect. Our progress was due to consistent effort by everyone right down the line, meeting competition, bringing forward new products, assailing new markets. Business is never easy, but some periods are rather less fraught than others.

U.K. steel production crashes in 1980 but we get by

With the arrival of the eighties our thermocouple business entered a very different climate. The economic wind veered to the north and frost and blizzards struck British industry and indeed the whole world. During the year 1980 the output of British manufacturing industry fell nearly 20% and crude steel production fell from 21.5 to 11.3 million tons. It recovered to remain around 15 million tons a year until 1987. Fortunately the steel

THE ELECTRONITE CONNECTION

works tended to reduce the size of each load rather than cut the number of heats melted, so our sale of liquid steel thermocouples fell rather less severely than the tonnage of steel melted and the business continued to remain profitable at a lower level of sales.

It is easy to give too much attention to the "bottom line" and to assume that all is well if the business is profitable. Staff reductions were made very skilfully and things looked fine. But there was one ominous fact that was far more important than current good profitability. The last British patent on liquid steel thermocouples would run out in 1982 and we were selling them at prices nearly double the prices ruling in Europe. When competition swept in from Europe our thermocouple business could have been swept away, and it very nearly happened. The final episodes of the story of Land Pyrometers will have to be told in Chapter 8.

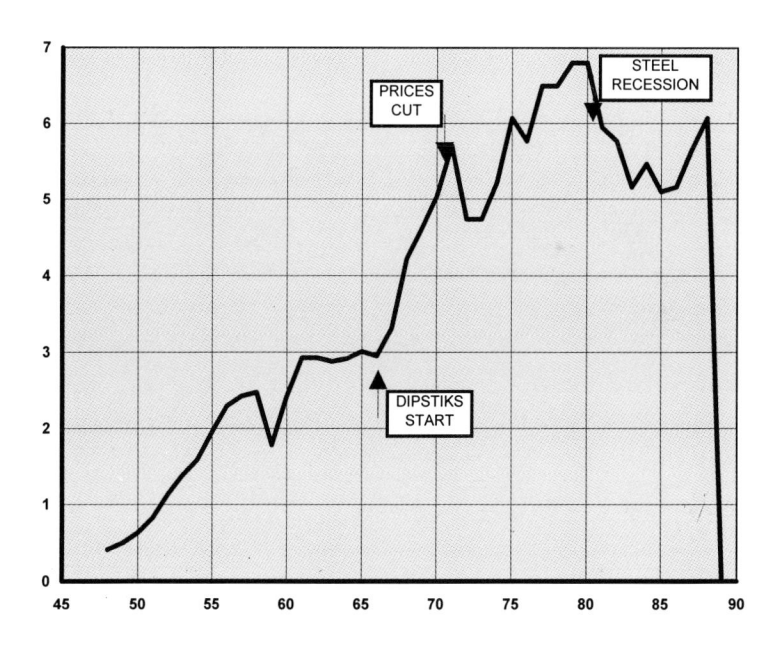

Fig. 4.3 The thermocouple sales of Land Pyrometers

The graph shows the sales of Land Pyrometer products including ElectroNite products. It also shows that in March 1989 the part of the business that included all thermocouples and other ElectroNite products had to be sold to ElectroNite. At that point Land Pyrometers joined T. Land & Son Ltd to become part of our history. It was an extremely important part of that history, a bridge across which we were able to pass from being manufacturers of silver plated tableware to the utterly different role of manufacturers of industrial measuring instruments.

CHAPTER 5
RADIATION PYROMETERS AT QUEENS ROAD
1950 to 1963

The roots of the new business that I started after the war all lay in the work that I had carried out at Jessops during the five years I that worked there for Donald Oliver. The first large project that I undertook for him was the conversion of the method of liquid steel temperature measurement invented by Schofield and Grace into a practical workshop tool. Out of that work there emerged the business that became Land Pyrometers. My second project at Jessops was the improvement of existing designs of radiation pyrometers. When our thermocouple business began to be profitable I turned my attention increasingly to radiation thermometry. This was a subject that I found fascinating and I must admit that the time that I spent on it at Queens Road was quite out of proportion to the immediate financial return. It was part business, part hobby and I enjoyed it immensely. In the end it has turned out to be the largest and most successful part of our business. Perhaps the moral is that you should do what you enjoy. I have tried to trace some of the key decisions that we took and give you a flavour of the sort of work that you do in such a business.

The Land Surface Pyrometer

For the first few years I had no time for such frivolities. The old electroplate and pewter business had to be kept going and be first underpinned then replaced by the new business in thermocouples and spares. But I still hankered to get back to radiation pyrometry; so when I heard in 1950 that the British Iron and Steel Research Association (BISRA) had taken up my invention of a surface pyrometer incorporating a reflecting hemisphere I had to find some way of getting in on the act.

The solution to my problem came to me over the telephone. When I was at Jessops I had had the good fortune to have working for me an excellent young man called Roy Barber. After the war he went to Sheffield University and took a degree in physics and did a bit of work at Queens Road during the vacations. One day I had a phone call from Roy saying that he had got his degree and asking me for a reference. I asked him if he would like a job and after some hesitation he decided to come and join us - just for a year! I promptly sent him off to London for 4 months to join the BISRA team working on the surface pyrometer. When he returned we set about designing the instrument that would be our first radiation pyrometer. Fred Nickols was working for us and he provided many good ideas for the mechanical design, which is still very little changed after 40 years.

BISRA had used a thermopile as the detector in their version of my surface pyrometer and I decided to do the same. We knew that the NPL had learnt during the war how to make thermopiles for military purposes. Fortunately I had friends at the NPL who gave us the right introductions to their colleagues. I must explain that a thermopile is an array of thermocouples connected in series to give a much larger output. In a radiation detector the thermocouples are not wires but very thin strips laid side by side and painted black to absorb as much radiant heat as possible.

The principle is illustrated in Fig. 5.1 where the two different metals forming the thermocouple are shown black and white respectively. The strips were only about half a millimetre wide. We used strips of manganin and constantan which we had sent away to be rolled as thin as possible on a special little rolling mill. Care was taken to keep the cold junctions (shown on the diagram as lying on the ring between the two circles) all at the same temperature as the surroundings of the thermopile. The hot junctions were free to be heated by the radiant heat incident on them to a temperature a degree or two above the surroundings. The output of the thermopile is, of course, a measure of the intensity of the incident radiation.

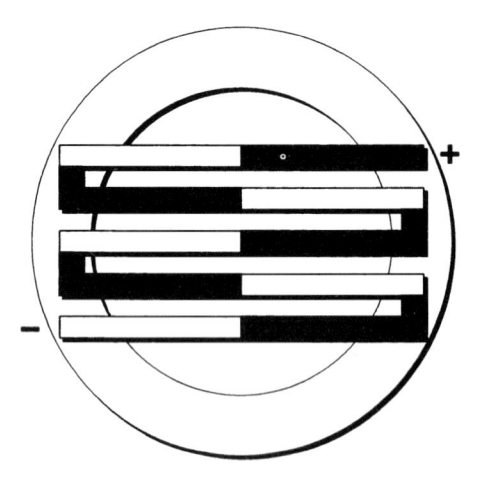

Fig. 5.1 Diagram of a thermopile

The success of the hemispherical mirror in producing black body conditions within it depends critically on the reflectivity of its metal surface. We decided to have it plated with a thick layer of gold which has a high reflectivity in the infrared part of the spectrum and is resistant to tarnishing. We provided the mirror with a dust cover to keep it clean when not in use. Fig. 5.2 shows how the pyrometer head was free to swivel at the end of a long telescopic handle. The cable from the pyrometer was connected to a portable galvanometer calibrated in temperature.

RADIATION PYROMETERS AT QUEENS ROAD

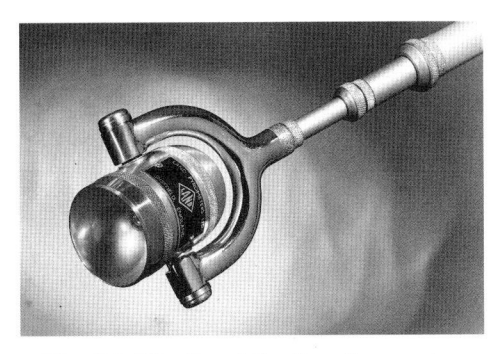

Fig. 5.2 The Land Surface Pyrometer

As well as designing the surface pyrometer we went to a lot of trouble to design a hot surface of known temperature that could be used to calibrate our instrument. We studied the theory of the pyrometer in great detail. It was something unique and we were determined that it should be of the finest class.

Fig. 5.3 I explain our surface pyrometer to the Master Cutler at our very first exhibition. The tubular figure was designed to 'hold' the pyrometer. The 'ingot' was very realistic and incorporated a hot plate that could be used to demonstrate the use of the pyrometer.

Roy Marsh was delighted to have the new pyrometer to sell. My father had taught me that when visiting a customer I should always try to have something new to show him. This was something new indeed; Roy was able to visit any steelworks in the world and know that he would be well received. The customer would be intrigued by the new pyrometer and off they would go into the works to try it out. There would soon be an order and Roy would have achieved the respect and often the friendship of a new customer.

A radiation pyrometer for Kents

In the summer of 1951 Jasmine was a baby. I had to go to London on some business trip so I took Audrey, Celia and baby Jasmine and we drove, on a very hot day, to stay for a couple of nights at Richmond. I had decided to call in on the way home at George Kent's at Luton to visit Reg Medlock. It was to be just a quick visit, but one thing led to another. Before long Reg was asking if we could make a radiation pyrometer for them to sell with their recorders. He was concerned that when they sold a pyrometer system for a steel-melting furnace they had to specify Honeywell pyrometers although Honeywell were their principal competitors. While we talked, my family were sitting in the car in the car-park being very good. When we had finished our discussion Reg and his colleagues took us all out for lunch at a local restaurant (I remember finding a live earwig in my raspberries!). By the time we got away the afternoon was well advanced and I was glad that we had had the foresight to put an extra feed for Jasmine's bottle in a vacuum flask. The bad news was that when we tried to use it we found that the milk had curdled and we drove home with a very hungry, and loudly protesting, future Managing Director.

It took some time to decide the design of the pyrometer for Kents. At Jessops we had in the library a book entitled "Temperature, its Measurement and Control in Science and Industry", which was a collection of papers presented at a conference in America in 1941. I bought a copy for myself. It was the first of a series that has continued every few years, a gold-mine of precious information and a constant up-dating of advances in temperature measurement world-wide. That first book contained a detailed description of the Honeywell Radiamatic Pyrometer and I studied it with the greatest care. I decided to use the Honeywell design as my starting-point. It was the best existing pyrometer and I wanted Kents, who were using Honeywells, to be able to change to Lands with a minimum of trouble. I used the same dimensions, the same focal length and the same diameter for the lens, the same field stop diameter, the same lens materials. But in other respects ours would be different.

I wanted to make big improvements in my new pyrometer. I wanted to make a pyrometer whose accuracy would at least match the accuracy of a base-metal thermocouple, a pyrometer that could be replaced by another if it were damaged, without readjustment of the measuring system. The disappearing filament optical pyrometer was a highly accurate instrument, used not only for industrial measurements but actually to define the International Temperature Scale at high temperatures. Industrial radiation pyrometers that were then available, although mechanically well designed, were not made to anything like the same precision of calibration. They were accepted as rather crude devices, used only when nothing better could be used. I decided that we would design a new breed of accurate radiation pyrometers.

A stable zero

The first requirement of a good radiation thermometer is a stable zero. This means the instrument gives no output at all when it is pointed at a cold surface. When an instrument is used to measure low temperatures such as 0 to 100°C it is necessary to define what you mean by a 'cold' surface very carefully. A poor instrument will give an output that drifts when the temperature of the instrument itself varies. Our surface pyrometer is placed directly on the hot surface, so we had had plenty of experience with the problem of drift. When we came to design a Pyrometer for Kents our first thought was to give it a stable zero and we were able produce a very stable pyrometer.

Getting rid of glare

I knew that existing pyrometers suffered from glare. When the pyrometer is sighted on a small hot surface a small pencil of radiation is focused on the detector through the field stop. But if the hot surface is large, a hundred times more radiation may also enter the body of the pyrometer and be reflected back and forth from the interior surfaces of the body. So the detector "sees" not only a bright lens but also the interior of the pyrometer illuminated by radiation reflected around inside. This is the source of 'glare' which produces an output dependent not only on the temperature of the hot surface that is being measured, but also on its size.

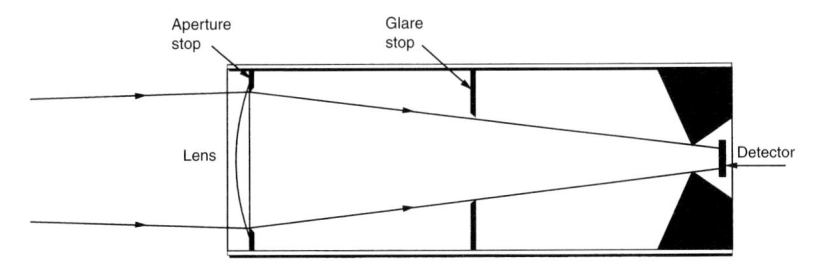

Fig. 5.4 A glare stop prevents the detector from receiving radiation reflected from inside surfaces reaching the detector.

After much thought we decided that we needed a glare stop, an extra aperture placed mid-way between the lens and the detector. Additionally, if all interior surfaces are painted with a first-class matt black paint, then a single glare-stop does the job.

The spherical calibrating furnace

A radiation pyrometer needs an accurate calibrating source with a large aperture. An optical pyrometer can easily be calibrated by sighting it into a small tube in a furnace held at a very uniform temperature, sometimes immersed in an ingot of melting metal. A radiation pyrometer needs a furnace with an aperture some 50 mm diameter. We were lucky that BISRA had devised a new source of black-body radiation that we could adopt (Fig. 5.5). It was a spherical furnace that could easily be maintained at a uniform temperature, whose characteristics could readily be calculated mathematically. We gratefully adopted the BISRA furnace design which gave us a unique capability to calibrate our pyrometers with high precision.

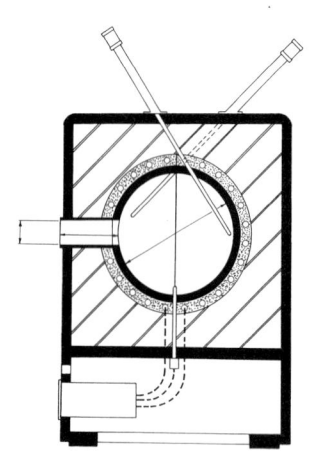

Fig. 5.5 The Spherical Black body that BISRA designed.

As well as being accurate a pyrometer needs to be convenient to use. Kents wanted a pyrometer for open-hearth furnaces so we went back to Jessops who let us build one for their furnace which I knew well. Measurement of the temperature of the inside of the furnace roof was an important project because it was all too easy to melt the silica bricks of which the roof was built. It was also a difficult measurement. It is a good idea to design an instrument for the most difficult application. Many of the sound features that we introduced into our design arose from the need to meet the difficult conditions of service at Jessops.

RADIATION PYROMETERS AT QUEENS ROAD

I knew that the pyrometry department would want to be able to check the accuracy of the pyrometer against a disappearing filament pyrometer. We therefore made it easy to remove the pyrometer and look down the line of sight. We made a separate mounting jacket that could be bolted in place and arranged for the pyrometer to slip into the jacket and clip into position without using tools. I knew it would be hot and uncomfortable where the pyrometer was mounted, so I provided a plug, not the convential screw terminals, for the connecting leads. I chose an American plug that was available worldwide. I knew that the lens would get dirty and might be splashed with hot metal, so I fitted a window in front of the lens and made it easy to remove the window and replace it if necessary.

Computer software is sometimes claimed to be "user-friendly". That describes exactly what we set out to achieve in all our designs. Some of the mountings that we designed are illustrated in Fig. 5.6. It is a tribute to our early design that it lasted essentially unchanged for 35 years; indeed an American competitor has recently copied it!

Learning to manufacture instruments

Our next task was to acquire and teach the new skills that we would need to become instrument manufacturers. First we had to learn to make a thermopile, the essential radiation detector that lay at the heart of not only the surface pyrometer but also the "Type R" radiation pyrometer that we designed for Kents. We knew that the National Physical Laboratory had needed to make thermopiles during the war. We went to see them and they showed us the practical techniques that they had developed. Then we had to train someone to do the job and Peggy Butcher became our first thermopile maker.

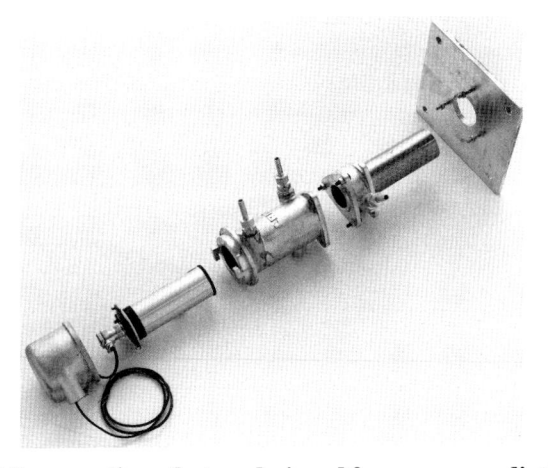

Fig. 5.6 Some of the mountings that we designed for our new radiation pyrometers.

We needed instrument makers. Fortunately the need for them arose at the time when we were selling the pewter business and Ron Short and Bill Roberts, who were our two most skilled metalsmiths, soon adapted their skills to building radiation pyrometers. We set up a calibration laboratory in a little room half way up the stairs over the garage, that had been the packing shop. There we installed Dick Nicholson with his calibration equipment - calibrated hot-plate for the surface pyrometers and spherical black-body furnaces for the Type R pyrometers. Dick was for many years the bed-rock of our business. Nothing that was not exactly right was allowed out of his department and in later years a succession of young men passed through his hands and learned the right tradition of accuracy and perfection.

The range of pyrometers expands

Roy Barber likes to quote a saying to the effect that "no sooner do you do more than they asked you to do than they expect you to do more than you do". This is just as true of customers as it is of bosses! Type R would measure temperatures down to about 600°C. Very soon we found a demand for the measurement of lower temperatures, which required the use of other lens materials, first silica (Type RS) then fluorite (Type RF). We soon found that fluorite had too much dispersion and it had to be replaced by arsenic trisulphide. Some applications needed to sight on smaller hot surfaces than Type R would accommodate and we made Type RN and Type RH. So our range of instruments grew and grew, every one being a small modification of something that we had made before, all using most of the same parts and looking very much alike.

We have always sought to establish close working relationships with companies of the highest calibre. Pilkington Brothers were then developing their revolutionary new 'float glass' process. When we showed them our surface pyrometer they wanted us to adapt it to measure the surface temperature of glass. Glass is strange stuff. It is transparent to visible light and to infrared radiation of short wavelengths, but at longer wavelengths it becomes completely opaque and almost perfectly black. So we had a go at making our surface pyrometer respond only to these long wavelengths. We no longer needed to fit a reflecting hemisphere, but we replaced the thermopile by a matched pair of thermopiles connected in opposition. We then placed a filter between them that would transmit the wavelengths that we wished to eliminate. After many struggles we managed to make this rather outlandish device work quite well. Thus we began a very fruitful association with some very pleasant and competent people. We were accepted as virtually part of the Pilkington Brothers Research Department and worked with them on the problems of glass temperature measurement. As they developed their wonderful new float-glass process we developed equipment for them to measure the temperatures throughout the process.

The international dimension

Our thermocouple business turned out to be very much a local business confined to the United Kingdom. The radiation pyrometer business was very different. We had equipment that we could sell all over the world and before long we had distributors in Australia and Sweden, France and Italy.

Our friends at Pilkingtons discussed our instruments with some of their foreign visitors and they came to see us. So it came about that I was invited in 1953 to give a lecture in Charleroi on pyrometers for glass and other surfaces. I decided to go on from Charleroi to have a holiday in France, so Audrey, Celia and Jasmine came too. I had my talk translated into French and learned it pretty well by heart on the plane. As I was delivering the lecture in my best French, Audrey and the girls walked past the open door and Jasmine was amazed. "Daddy's going jabber, jabber, jabber!" I managed the lecture quite nicely, but I had not reckoned with the questions, which came thick and fast - in French. I had, a little shamed-facedly, to ask for translations.

Our principal customer in France was La Pyrometrie Industrielle, a firm in Paris manufacturing temperature indicators and recorders. The head of the firm was André Fridberg who was keenly interested in radiation pyrometry and who came over to Queens Road to receive a detailed course of instruction, chiefly from me. Fortunately he spoke excellent English, having been brought up by an English nanny. We became very good friends and kept in touch until his death at the age of 97.

In 1956 the Sheffield Smelting Company, who made platinum-rhodium thermocouple wires for us, passed on to us an enquiry from a Japanese firm in Osaka called Kawaso. They wanted, I think, some thermocouple sheaths and we were able to supply what they required. We gave them also the details of all the other things that we made and then began an astonishing association. Whatever new thing we made they ordered and began to sell. With Japanese thoroughness they mastered the technical details that we sent them and their file was quite unique among our distributors. All other distributors had thick, fat correspondence files and slim order files. Kawaso had a slim correspondence file and a nice thick order file. Before long Japan became our largest export market. Roy Barber went over to visit Kawaso and talk to their customers. Over the years Roy kept in touch with our friends in Japan. By visits, lectures, and personal contacts he nurtured this precious, vigorous and exotic plant that had come our way. We learned later that in certain Japanese steelworks a radiation pyrometer became known as a "LAND". There's fame for you! Kawaso remained our distributors for 40 years.

Another successful distributor that we found in the early days was Duff and Macintosh who represented us in Australia. Duff and Mac was run by a wonderful character by the name of Kitchener ("Kitch") Nolan. We would get not only business correspondence and orders, but also frequent cuttings from newspapers and magazines with jokes and funnies of all kinds. Kitch was a great character and we entertained him and his wife on many occasions. We also did a nice bit of business.

Getting started in America

In 1953 I went to Manchester to visit the firm of Fielden Instruments and met Jack Fielden. His family were in textiles, but he was not interested in the old business, his interest was electronics. He had invented a new capacitative level gauge for measuring the level of liquids and powders in industrial processes. He had established a small plant in Philadelphia to cover the American market.

He was interested in our surface pyrometer, not to sell in England, but as a possible new product for his American Company. He asked if we were selling in America and I said no. When he suggested that his American company might sell it, I said "Why not?" and we made a deal. In fact he had sold the controlling interest in his American company to Robertshaw Fulton but he retained an interest and was able to arrange for them to be our distributors.

In 1954 Roy Barber and I had published a paper in England on the theory of the suction pyrometer. In 1956 I was invited to read a paper on the same subject at the Pittsburg meeting of the Instrument Society of America. It was a trip that I remember vividly. In those days transatlantic flights were only just possible in propeller driven aircraft. I went to London Airport where there was a collection of huts on the edge of the airport that served as the terminal for flights to America. I arrived in the evening and set off in darkness. First we flew to Shannon in Eire where the fuel tanks were topped up and I wandered round the Duty Free Shop. Then we flew on to Gander in Newfoundland where we got out into the snow while they re-fuelled again. Finally we flew down the coast of North America to Idlewild airport (now J.F.Kennedy).

The flight was long, noisy and cramped and I arrived in New York very tired and rather disoriented. I managed to pick up a bus to La Guardia. I was taken aback by the roads with 4 lanes in each direction and the big American cars speeding along. Air travel was all very new to me but I managed to find my way onto the correct plane. This little plane took us down to Philadelphia and then west over the Allegheny mountains to Pittsburg. It was a bumpy ride over the mountains. I had eaten nothing since breakfast and I begged a couple of biscuits from the air hostess. As we came in to land in the unpressurized plane I had the most excruciating pain in my ears. At last I reached the hotel and went down to dinner relishing the thought of a good meal and a glass of wine. But it was Sunday and no alcohol was allowed. So this was America!

I meet Fred Maltby

Fieldens had arranged a little exhibition stand and I was interviewed briefly on local radio. Ralph Coles, who was in charge of the Fielden operation, met me and looked after me very well. The lecture went well, but in the evening I was taken violently ill, either due to the flight or something I had eaten. Ralph was very kind and in the

RADIATION PYROMETERS AT QUEENS ROAD

morning I was fit to go on to Philadelphia. Ralph Coles introduced me to Fred Maltby who was Fielden's head of research and development. I shook hands with a big, smiling, cigar-smoking man with a twinkle in his eye and a limp caused by boyhood polio.

Fig. 5.7 Fred Maltby.

We liked and respected each other at once and we have been good friends ever since. Within quite a short time Robertshaws decided to move the Fielden operation to the west coast. Fred Maltby decided it was a good time to start something on his own and he set up as a consultant in Philadelphia. We arranged that he should act as our agent in America and I sent Roy Marsh out with a set of radiation pyrometer samples. They put the samples in the back of Fred's car and set off across America to visit potential customers. Fred wisely chose chiefly to visit instrument companies that did not manufacture radiation pyrometers of their own. The business that resulted was not enormous but it helped Fred to pay the rent and it gave us a toe-hold in America.

Fig. 5.8 Roy Marsh showing a Land Surface Pyrometer to a customer in America.

Don Nielsen begins to sell Land products

During their travels they met Don Neilsen who was setting up on his own just outside New York as Atlantic Pyrometers to import and distribute equipment chiefly from England. Our products were included among the lines that he sold. Unfortunately for Don, all the other products that he chose were unsuccessful, so he was left trying to make a living selling Land products. This was not easy for him because the unit price of a radiation pyrometer was relatively modest and the knowledge needed to sell it was formidable; but he worked hard and had some success.

Travelling the great American highways

After Roy Marsh left I took the American market under my wing. We sold to instrument companies directly. Most other business went through Atlantic Pyrometers who had a non-exclusive right to sell in the U.S.A. and an exclusive agreement for surface pyrometers. Audrey went with me once or twice a year and we travelled around with Fred Maltby. It was not easy for her to leave the children, but she came along and was a great help to me and enjoyed the trips. Other people such as Roy Barber and Mike Rucklidge also went over quite frequently. It was moderately successful for us, moderately successful for Don Nielsen and a bit untidy but it was all that we could do at that time. It was frustrating to see the great American market and to be able to do so little there.

Audrey and I had a wonderful guide in Fred. He was our chauffeur; we would hire a car at the airport and pile in, sitting three abreast in the front seat, and drive off along the great American freeways. You must remember that when we first went to America the total motorway system of the U.K. consisted of the M1 from London to Birmingham and a bit of the M6 north of Manchester. In America there were thousands and thousands of miles of wonderful roads. Fred took us to see supermarkets and discount stores - a new way of shopping that we had never seen. We went to steak-houses, we ate popcorn and drank Coke and we stayed overnight in motels where you drove your car up to your room and unpacked your luggage straight in. It was a completely new world in those days, a preview of the future.

As we drove along, Fred would tell us all about the country we were driving through. I remember in New York State stopping by a sign at the roadside where Fred explained about the porterage system in the days of the canals. We would also talk business. Fred explained the rep system that covers America. In the instrument business there was (and still is) an invaluable network of manufacturers' representatives each of whom sells the products of perhaps half a dozen manufacturers in a limited area. The secret of successful selling is to attract and motivate a band of good reps covering the country who are keen to sell your products. Fred would tell me stories about his reps and the best ways to motivate them to give attention to your products rather than someone else's. We would also talk about technical problems. Fred is an exceptionally clever electrical engineer and we would talk about the application of electronics to our pyrometers. The transistor was just coming over the horizon in those years and we had ideas about using transistors to extend the capabilities of our instruments. So with Fred Maltby and Don Nielsen we made a start in the American market.

When Roy Marsh left and we reorganized the business I had refused to cut back on our research and development program. As business improved in 1960 we had begun to add to our staff of physicists. It was around that time that Percy Wilenski and Michael Rucklidge had joined us. Mike had been a school teacher and then moved to the British Coke Research Association. One day he was laying the fire with newspaper and sticks, and noticed an advertisement in the paper he was using, for a physicist at Land Pyrometers. He decided to go and see what it was about, decided to join us and stayed until he retired. Both Mike and Percy were great acquisitions.

The silicon "solar" cell - wow!

When I was at Jessops I had been greatly impressed by the possibilities of using a selenium photoelectric cell as the radiation detector in place of the traditional thermopile. It had a perfectly stable zero and a very high speed of response and it responded only to visible light. At such wavelength there was no absorption of radiation by water vapour in the atmosphere and errors arising from uncertainty about the reflective properties of the surface were substantially reduced. I modified the Type R pyrometer to use the selenium cell, but the range of useful applications was severely limited.

In 1959 I went to an exhibition organized by the Physical Society and there I saw for the first time a silicon solar cell. These cells had been developed to convert sunlight into electrical power for space vehicles. I could see that they might be used as detectors in radiation pyrometers so I obtained samples to test. The best cells were from Ferranti. When we ran our tests we were over the moon. These cells were phenomenal, they might have been invented specially for radiation pyrometry. They were incredibly fast in response - we could not measure their speed for some years but it turned out to be of the order of a millionth of a second. They were much more sensitive then selenium cells and they did not suffer from the problem of drift. The zero of the cell was rock steady and it could be operated in ambient temperatures of 100°C and more. We knew at once that these cells would transform the science of radiation pyrometry.

We made our first demonstration pyrometer for Jackson Brothers (glass manufacturers) in January 1960 and called it Type RR. It was able to measure temperatures down to about 650°C. Its range of sensitivity (about 0.5 to 1.0 micrometers) was ideal for pyrometry, avoiding all water-vapour and CO_2 absorption bands in the atmosphere. The great sensitivity of the cell allowed us to measure much smaller targets. It gave us an instrument with most of the benefits of the disappearing filament optical pyrometer but with the great advantage that it needed no operator. It would give a continuous output that could be displayed on a recorder or indicator. We called it the Continuous Optical Pyrometer. Today silicon cell pyrometers are used world-wide for the great majority of high temperature measurements.

I considered the possibility of patenting the use of a silicon cell in radiation thermometry, but I was very doubtful whether the use of yet another different photocell in a radiation pyrometer was a patentable invention. I decided that the important need was to prevent anyone else from claiming prior publication of the idea. At the time we were very inexperienced in the field of patents and totally unaware of American law and practice. To establish our claim to be the first in the field Roy Barber and I published a paper in the next book in the series "Temperature, its Measurement and Control in Science and Industry". The paper was entitled "The Place of Photovoltaic Detectors in Temperature Measurement".

The turbine blade pyrometer

The silicon cell arrived just in time for our development program with Rolls Royce. We had sold thermocouples and protection tubes to Rolls Royce for some years and they knew of our activities in radiation pyrometry. One day in 1961 they came to see us with a new idea. They had patented the idea of a radiation pyrometer to measure the temperature of the rotor blades in an aircraft gas turbine. They wanted us to make an experimental pyrometer for them. Our response was to persuade them that they should abandon the thermopile detector that they had intended to use and to adopt the new silicon solar cell instead. So we began a 20 year development programme that finally came to fruition in the pyrometers that are fitted to the RB 199 engines which power the Tornado fighter aircraft. By the time we moved to Dronfield our little business in infrared thermometers represented just a quarter of our sales. But it was profitable, it was growing at 20% a year and I judged that it had a good future.

CHAPTER 6
BIGGER SIGNALS, BIGGER SALES
1964 to 1983

The move to Dronfield

When we moved to Dronfield the radiation pyrometer business was a serious part of our business and I gave careful attention to its needs. I decided that the Research Department needed a new name to reflect its increasingly commercial importance. It became the Product Development Department, which exactly described what it did. The big room upstairs was set aside for a laboratory which housed both the Calibration Department and the Product Development Department, which is illustrated as it looked in 1969 in Fig. 6.1. Graham Torr is standing at the back, talking to Bernard Jarman and David Cresswell, Dave Brett in the centre, Mike Rucklidge is peering through an eye-piece at something (I wonder what?) and John Ellis in the foreground.

Fig. 6.1 The Product Development Laboratory in 1969.

You may notice the benches which I designed specially. Each includes two optical benches comprising a long steel rod about 4cm diameter pointing towards a spherical furnace and recessed flush with the bench surface. Special clamps to hold the pyrometers were designed, each with two V contacts straddling the steel rod and a single point contact on the surface of the bench leaving a single degree of freedom of movement directed to the opening in the furnace. This arrangement gave us a clear bench surface which was a great convenience in the days when measuring instruments were much bigger than they are today.

Capturing the fleeting signal

The silicon cell was a godsend. Traditional radiation thermometers were rather slow in response (about 2 seconds) and limited in their sensitivity. There was constant pressure from customers to provide thermometers that would measure smaller targets and lower temperatures and respond faster. The silicon cell gave us a big improvement in sensitivity when measuring high temperatures and almost unlimited speed of response. Unfortunately it was not so easy to make use of the fast response because the recorders that were available were not fast enough to respond to the signal. Driving through America with Fred Maltby, we discussed the problem and Fred said "What we need is a peak-picker". A peak-picker would catch the fleeting peak signal and store it for long enough for a recorder to respond or until the thermometer had another brief glimpse of the hot surface.

Bigger signals

So we found ourselves moving into the world of electronics, where transistors were taking over from the old thermionic valves. In everyday speech a transistor usually means a neat little radio, but the transistor radio takes its name from the tiny electrical device that makes the radio work. Its job is to take the very small electric currents that are picked up by the aerial and amplify them into much larger currents that will drive the loud speaker. The amplifier needs several transistors to do the job. We needed a very stable transistor amplifier that would deal satisfactorily with very small direct currents. The current from the silicon cell in the radiation thermometer might be only one millionth of an ampere. We needed to amplify it up to perhaps a thousandth of an ampere. At that level of current we could work in volts, not thousandths of a volt, and that would be big enough to feed into a peak-picker. We found a transistor amplifier made in Germany by a firm called Knick that would do the job. By the time that we came to Dronfield we were supplying Knick amplifiers and developing peak-picking circuits for the more difficult applications.

The "parrot's perch" experiment

In 1965 we decided to find out which was the most accurate method of measuring the temperature of hot steel strip in a rolling mill. The measurement is a difficult one but very important in running a rolling mill. The steel billets came out of the re-heating furnace bright red hot and covered in scale. Most of the scale fell off in the roughing process, but patches of scale remained. The moving steel was sprayed with water, producing clouds of steam, and pools of water might run along on the surface of the steel. With pools of water and patches of scale covering parts of the hot steel the indicated temperature fluctuated substantially. The highest readings represented the true temperature of the steel.

We thought that a silicon cell pyrometer with a peak-picker should be the best choice for rolling mills but we decided to settle the matter by a carefully controlled experiment. The management of the rolling mill at Steel Peach and Tozer at Rotherham allowed us to set up four different recording systems looking at the same area of steel in the rolling mill. The four pyrometers sat on a T-shaped mounting of steel tubing that became known as the "parrot's perch". They were:

> A conventional pyrometer using a thermopile detector (type ORO)
>
> A pyrometer using a silicon detector (Type OQO)
>
> A similar pyrometer with a Knick Amplifier and a peak-picker
>
> A "ratio" pyrometer that measured radiation in two different wavebands and deduced the temperature from the ratio of the two outputs. This is sometimes called a colour pyrometer. Before pyrometers were used experienced furnacemen used to judge the temperature of red-hot steel chiefly by its colour.

We also used a Land Surface Pyrometer to measure the true temperature; of course this gave us only "spot" readings, not a continuous record. A major objective of this important experiment was to see whether we were right to reject the popular belief that ratio thermometers were the answer to most problems in radiation thermometry. It gave us reassurance on this point.

The "parrot's perch experiment" demonstrated that it was best to use a peak-picking circuit in conjunction with a silicon cell pyrometer. So when we received an order for the new computer-controlled rolling mill at Dorman Long's Lackenby Works we decided to fit amplifiers and peak pickers. It was nearly a disaster.

Putting an amplifier in the thermometer head

Fortunately we had just engaged a very competent and thorough physicist called Keith Moore who was in charge of the installation. The amplifiers and peak-pickers had been installed in the computer-room, which was some hundreds of metres away from the pyrometer. The connecting cables ran through an underground passage-way with all the electrical cables for the mill. The result was that the 20 millivolt signal from the pyrometer was accompanied by 8 volts of noise picked up from the power cables! The peak picker was swamped by the transient noise. Keith realized that he no longer had the long time-constant of the recorder to smooth out the transients arising from electrical interference. He transferred the Knick amplifiers to a waterproof box very close to the thermometers and re-routed the signal cables well away from the power cables. Screened leads were used for the low-power signals from the thermometers. The results were excellent.

The work at Lackenby finished in early 1966. It had taught us again that we needed to work in volts, but now we knew that we must also find a way to put the amplifier inside the thermometer head. Within a year or two we were able to buy operational amplifiers made on single silicon chips and sealed in small cans which made that feasible. Also the field-effect transistor came on the market enabling us to make much improved peak-pickers. We were moving into a new generation of radiation thermometers that worked in volts.

ElectroNite become our distributors

Before we moved to Dronfield I had realized that we needed our own office in America and in May 1963 I had offered to buy Atlantic Pyrometers. Don Nielsen was by then selling only Land products and finding it hard to succeed with limited resources. By August we had agreed in principle that we would do so. But Don was a stubborn man who desperately wanted to succeed in a business of his own and he kept putting off the actual sale despite generous offers. In May 1966 Larry Littman came to see us, proposing that Land and ElectroNite should extend our basis of co-operation. After some hesitation I decided that they might be able to do a better job for us in the States and that if Don was agreeable to move we would try it. He moved very reluctantly from the north side of New York city to North Philadelphia and went to work for ElectroNite.

We win the Armco competition

The arrangement was certainly not my greatest idea but it did turn up a very important enquiry. ElectroNite reported in 1967 that Armco Steel in Middletown, Ohio were about to conduct a contest to find the most suitable range of radiation thermometers for

BIGGER SIGNALS, BIGGER SALES

a new computer-controlled mill that Kaiser Engineering were about to install. We were just reaching the point of putting an amplifier in the head of a pyrometer when I heard the news. I insisted that we should get into this trial and win the order. With the parrot's perch trial to go by and our experience at Lackenby I reckoned that we would leave the competition standing. Roy Barber and Keith flew out to visit Armco (it was almost too late) and persuaded them to include our equipment in this trial.

Heart in mouth, Keith Moore sent off the very first of our new 'J' range of thermometers, that had at last got an amplifier in the thermometer head, and a peak-picker. Our system won the competition, ironically less on its technical features than on the practical grounds that the Land "wrap-around" jacket, allowing easy replacement and cleaning of the thermometer, was the best invention yet! The mighty Honeywell went so far as to supply a Honeywell thermometer adapted to fit in a Land jacket. It sounds all too easy, but here is Keith's personal account of the trip he made to attend the trials.

> 'In 1967 I left Land Pyrometers in early March bound for America and Armco. Crocuses, clustered on the lawn on Wreakes Lane, opened their faces to the bright spring sunshine and all was well with the world. In America they were having one of the worst winters for years. Russ Angers of ElectroNite and I ground our way through feet of snow to Middletown. The rolling mill was an awesome sight. Icicles, which had formed on the metalwork in the mill, melted as the hot steel passed and froze again as soon as it had gone by.
>
> 'Fred Richards and I installed a pyrometer in the mill, and to get cooling water to the jacket (I can't think why!), Fred held the end of a frozen water pipe and I played a blow-torch on the part above ground. In typical Laurel and Hardy fashion, Fred was caught unawares by the sudden freeing of the water supply and spent an uncomfortable half-hour crunching around in ice-laden trousers. The thermometer worked! Fred even invited me to a magnificent dinner at his home. I remember this as the first time I ate sweet potatoes - I thought the intense frost had attacked the carrots, to everyone's amusement.'

The thermometer we supplied had multiple temperature ranges and a particular range was selected by a clever wiring pattern in the loose connector associated with the thermometer. This allowed us to use one type of thermometer for all the different temperature ranges met with in hot steel rolling, simply by changing the wiring connections in the loose plug. Thus the customer needed to carry fewer spare thermometers. Kaiser Engineering were quite easily convinced to buy Land systems for Armco.

Later in 1967 we solved the problem of the lower temperatures that we met at the coilers. For this application we used a thermometer (Type OQM) incorporating an optical filter that eliminated most of the reflected daylight or shop lighting that interfered with the measurement. With a complete range of thermometers technically superior to our competitors we were able to sell systems to other rolling mills. Our systems were installed successfully at Asheville, Kentucky in 1968, for Cockeril at Liege and in several new mills installed by GEC Electrical Projects and Davy United.

Thus we managed to get our nose in front in the important market that was the world-wide steel industry. We were already establishing ourselves more firmly in the glass industry by developing a close relationship with the very progressive people at Corning Glass in New York State, who had been introduced to us by our friends at Pilkingtons. These two companies were world leaders in two sides of the glass industry, Pilkingtons in flat glass and Corning in special glasses. We have always found our greatest success by working with customers who are leaders in their particular industries.

EleectroNite widen their horizons

The arrangement for ElectroNite to sell our products in America was not successful. Our salesmen selling Dipstiks to British steelworks were able pick up orders for radiation thermometers while they were calling on their customers. I had hoped that ElectroNite salesmen might do the same in America. But they did not have the training, the contact with research and development or the motivation to make a success of the project. Furthermore I soon had reason to doubt Larry Littman's business judgement.

Larry had been phenomenally successful with liquid steel thermocouples and had built up a fine world-wide business in a very short time. He was a pioneer in global marketing of a single product in the instrument industry. He now made the same mistake that I had begun to make a few years before. He decided that he must extend his success into other areas of instrumentation. Land radiation thermometers were only a beginning. He built a big factory in Philadelphia and set about filling it with business. He found a clever engineer on the west coast who had invented a linear motor that could be adapted to drive the pen on a temperature recorder. It was a good idea and greatly simplified the design of recorders. Larry went into production and wanted us to sell the recorder in the U.K. and perhaps to manufacture it under licence.

We gave it a careful thought and decided that this was not for us. I was beginning to recognize that the secret of success in the instrument industry was going to lie in 'niche' marketing on a world-wide scale. Eric and I went to Philadelphia and saw the vast new factory and talked to Larry. I remember telling Larry that I felt that it was a mistake to challenge the big manufacturers on their own ground. I said "If I had a little goat I would tether it safely in a corner of the meadow where the grass was lush and green, where the bigger animals did not bother to go." He was not impressed but my judgement was soon vindicated.

ElectroNite in trouble

In the Autumn of 1970 I was visiting North America with Audrey. I was talking to Leigh Instruments in Ottawa and got wind of the fact that ElectroNite were running into a lot of trouble. Some of their better people were leaving and one in particular, Mark Laudermilk, was setting up a new company in Canton Ohio. Mark had been one of Larry's best people. I decided to visit Mark and find out what was happening.

The trouble was serious and it looked as if ElectroNite might fall to pieces. Their big new ideas had produced big new expenses but no big new business. They were neglecting quality control and customer service in their thermocouple business in America. As a result they were in serious financial difficulties. The company was saved by Henk Kleyn who was able to borrow $2 million in America on the strength of his personal track record in Europe and he set about putting the company right.

We decide to form our own company in U.S.A.

At the time I did not know which way things would go and I decided that we must get our radiation thermometer business out of the mess. So we went on to Philadelphia and took a suite at the Barclay Hotel in Ritter Square where we set about the job of establishing our own company. First we had Don Nielsen and Shirley to dinner where we discussed the ElectroNite situation. Don was horrified by the way the business was being run and was all for getting out at once. Then we had a long evening with Fred Maltby and Mildred and got a whole lot of good advice and useful contacts from Fred who was friendly and helpful as he always had been. I phoned Eric and he agreed that we must get on with the job. It seemed a bit mad to land ourselves with a new American Company just when Land Europe was getting off the ground, but it was the only thing to do.

By November 1970 Land Instruments Inc. was being formed and since I happened to be ill at the time it was Eric who went over to Philadelphia to meet Don and find a site for the new business. Eric and I then went to New York to interview candidates for the job of second-in-command to Don. We chose a young physicist called Ray Peacock, a charming fellow whom we liked very much and whose scientific knowledge would complement Don's experience as an instrument salesman. Unlike Land Europe, Land Instruments was a success. Sales in the first year were about £40,000 and within two years they had increased to nearly £130,000. Don was delighted to be back running his own little business; he had been miserable at ElectroNite.

Eric Land is appointed Managing Director but I remain an active chairman

We were entering a time of critical and difficult change in the business. I was aware that our management structure needed to be changed. In 1971 I came to the quite sensible conclusion that joint Managing Directors were nonsense. The only way out appeared to be for me to retire as a Managing Director and let Eric be sole Managing Director. I would remain an active chairman and continue to contribute substantially to the technical development of the infrared division. It was a rash decision to give Eric so much power at a time when it was impossible to foresee how the business would develop. A few years later it caused me great trouble because the business turned into something that Eric was quite unqualified to manage and I had a dreadful job recovering control of my business.

The development of System 2

In those days we did not yet sell a standard range of the more advanced products. We were using the new electronic components and our ingenuity to solve problems as our customers brought them to us. Out of this experience a new range of thermometers gradually emerged. It was clear at a fairly early stage that the new electronics was going to allow us to produce a linearized output from a radiation thermometer. It is an inconvenient fact of nature that the intensity of thermal radiation increases more and more steeply as the temperature of a hot surface rises. The output of the thermometer is far from a 'linear function' of temperature and is therefore unsuitable to feed into a digital indicator or a computer. One of the competing thermometers in the Armco trial had a crude linearizing circuit that made us sit up and think. As time went on amplifiers became better and cheaper and smaller, and soon we were able to make a linearizing circuit that was good enough to suit our exacting standards.

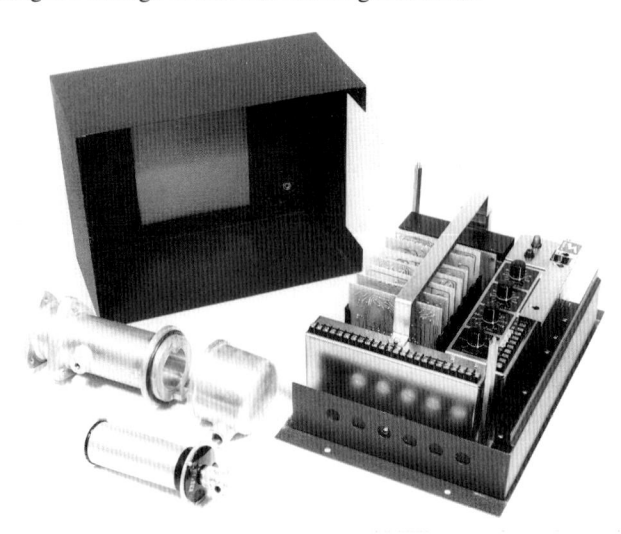

Fig. 6.2 System 2 thermometers and signal processing unit.

By 1972 we were able to introduce a range of new high-technology thermometers that we called System 2. It had thermometers with amplifiers incorporated in the head, which fitted in our standard wrap-around jackets. A separate signal-processing unit incorporated a linearizer and an optional selection of peak-pickers, averagers and sample-and-hold circuits. In December 1972 System 2 was turned over to production and the first systems came out of the production department and out to the customers. Electronics had become central to our products.

The optical system also needed to be put on a rational basis. I had time to spare so I took on that part of the job myself. I was so keen to make it totally rational and comprehensive that (as usual) I went a bit over the top. I had to take a firm line with myself and say "enough" in a very loud voice. We continued to polish the system and we eventually came up with System 2 Mark II. This was still abominably complicated, but at least rational if you took the trouble to understand it. Although Roy and I and others played our parts in the development of System 2 there is no doubt in my mind that it was essentially the creation of Keith Moore.

The Infrared Division gets its own Sales Department 1973

By the end of 1973 I had decided that it was time for the radiation thermometry division to have its own sales force. This was a very big and risky decision but a correct one. Until that time we had kept down the cost of selling radiation thermometers in the U.K. by using salesmen whose primary job was to sell thermocouples and accessories. By 1973 it was clear that this was no longer good enough.

The Infrared Division had become a business of a kind that was quite unlike either T. Land & Son Ltd. or Land Pyrometers, a business of a kind of which none of us had any experience. The market for which my father's electroplate and pewter business had catered in 1935 had been small and very simple. Half of the sales had gone to Boots the Chemists and most of the rest had gone through the hands of Mr. Pegler, who was a manufacturers' representative in London. Land Pyrometers was almost as simple as long as it was just a thermocouple business. Our main customers were the steel companies in the U.K. where we knew everybody who could give us a decent order, knew them well over a long time.

When we had added radiation thermometers, they had been sold at first to much the same customers in the U.K. But our market for infrared thermometers had gradually become an international one and now extended well beyond steel into such industries as glass, aero-engines, food, and plastics.

I put one of our most experienced salesman in charge of radiation thermometer sales. He had studied marketing and had ideas that might have been very beneficial but I slowly and very reluctantly came to the conclusion that he was not the right man for the job. To this day I cannot put my finger on the problem and say exactly what was lacking. He had many good qualities and good ideas but there was something missing in the area of authority and leadership. In the end I could not escape the conclusion that we would have to try again. As I had done once before, I took the job on myself until I could make better arrangements. For a few weeks I moved into the Infrared Sales Manager's office to keep things moving while I tried to work out how the business should develop. I remember sitting in that little office feeling a complete wally, wondering where on earth I should go from here.

Roy Barber takes control of Infrared Sales

Eventually I remembered my old guiding principle that it was my job to steer the business, not to pedal. A man of 60 did not have the energy to do all the things that would need to be done in this new emerging business. I had a much better man available. In 1974 I decided that I must expand Roy Barber's role to include sales and marketing as well as product development. It proved to be the right choice. I left Roy in charge of the radiation division, responsible to Eric. He appointed Dave Coe to be product development manager. I cheerfully set about completing a book on temperature measurement that I had been working on from time to time for many years.

The story of Roy Barber's twelve years in charge of the infrared thermometer business needs to be told all in one piece and you will find it in Chapter 9. I am skipping on a few years to tell you how Jasmine came to join the business in 1977. The transition from one generation to the next is often a stormy episode in a family business. This one was no exception.

CHAPTER 7
THE NEXT GENERATION - JASMINE JOINS THE BUSINESS
1977 to 1987

No one who lived and worked in England during the nineteen-seventies will forget the experience. We had strikes, we had power cuts, we sat freezing in our offices through the winter, we were even reduced to working a three-day week. Successive governments lost control of the Trades Unions, lost control of the economy and lost control of inflation which soared above 20% in 1976. We even bought a gas-powered electricity generator, though by the time it was installed and running the worst was over and we never used it. The Labour government introduced prices and incomes policies which were a farce and a disaster.

At Lands we were fortunate and we were successful and our profits, even after deducting the profit-sharing bonus, only once fell below 10% of sales. These profits were true profits, corrected for the massive distortions that arise when accountants are foolish enough to use historic cost accounting in times of high inflation. Sales of all products increased during the decade by 83% after making allowance for inflation. Despite high taxation we were able to retain enough of our profits in the business to double the shareholders' equity in real terms. Consequently we were in an exceptionally strong financial position in 1980, which turned out to be very fortunate indeed.

The burner control project

When I retired as Managing Director I had decided to complete a project that I had started of writing a first-class book about temperature measurement in industry and had settled down to finish my book at home. I dropped in at the works from time to time. One day in 1974 I found that there was an enquiry from Jim Swithenbank who was a lecturer (later professor) at the Fuel Technology department of Sheffield University. One of his PhD students had been measuring the variation in the infrared radiation emitted by a flame at various ratios of fuel flow to air flow. The measurements suggested that it might be possible to control the combustion of fuels by simple measurements of the radiation emitted by flames. They were being supported by a grant from Esso Research and they needed a further £2,000 to complete trials that were underway. Would we like to contribute a further £2,000 to complete the project?

I went to their laboratory up in the hills above Buxton to see for myself what they were doing. Their objective was simple and rather startling. When the fuel/air ratio was exactly right the temperature of the flame would be at the maximum possible level and the fuel consumption would be at the lowest possible value. There might be no need to measure the fuel flow or the air flow. It might be possible to achieve optimum efficiency just by measuring the radiation from the flame with one of our infrared thermometers. This would be rather something! I decide to invest the £2,000 that they needed and to ask permission to do a few trials on an industrial boiler at ICI Winnington in Cheshire. This was the beginning of the burner control project that was to tantalize us with intermittent success for several years. If it had really come off it would have been a big winner.

Jasmine joins the team working on Burner Control.

By the beginning of the seventies our second daughter Jasmine had collected enough O levels and good A levels to be offered a place at Oxford. She declined the offer on the reasonable grounds that she would have to work much too hard to keep up with all those clever people. She wanted to enjoy the social amenities offered by a university, so she went to Leicester instead and enjoyed it all. She narrowly escaped the indignity of getting a first in mathematics (which would have been most embarrassing) but easily

Fig. 7.1 Jasmine Harfoot.

THE NEXT GENERATION - JASMINE JOINS THE BUSINESS

achieved her goal of improving on my modest 2.2. She then decided to become a chartered accountant and subsequently went on to get a very good job as a management accountant at Boots the Chemists in their headquarters in Nottingham. This job gave her experience of a broad range of financial and associated management issues.

From odd comments that she had made I knew that she had an aversion to family businesses with their tendency to encourage nepotism and their potential for family feuds. But as she gathered experience of working in a big organization she began to wonder if a smaller firm might be more congenial. It might also be easier to overcome the obstacles that a woman found in big businesses. One day when we were discussing these matters she got round to wondering whether a career in the family business might suit her after all. Perhaps she would like to try it for a year? As we talked it over she decided that it might be a sensible idea, so I promised to talk to Eric about it. It would be no easy ride for her or for me.

When I mentioned Jasmine's interest in joining the firm Eric was doubtful whether there was any suitable position for her. I said that she could join the small team that was working on the burner control project and so in 1977 Jasmine started work learning the job from the bottom. When we decided to put our £2,000 on this horse we decided to put some of our best product development people on it too. Dave Coe was a physicist who came to us when he got his degree in physics at Oxford and Roy Barber had put him in charge of product development. With Roy's permission I had high-jacked him and put him in charge of what was to become the Combustion division. We picked out a few more likely lads including Martin Johnston and Mike Bray. Mike had recently arrived with a degree in electronic engineering. He belonged to the new generation who naturally solved their problems with a microprocessor or two. Jasmine acquired a hard hat, a boiler suit, industrial boots and a project of her own. She was to look at the special problems of small boilers with help from Dave Coe, Mike Bray and the team. A bit different from an accounts office.

We had no idea when we set up the Combustion Division that we were launching our little craft into such stormy seas. It was to swing from dizzy success to calamity, back and forth through the eighties and now the nineties. We have hung on, believing that in the end we shall be among the survivors in this important market, with a sound business and a seasoned crew. The story of the Combustion Division is the topic of Chapter 10.

In this chapter I want to tell you how we got out of the dreadful hole that I foolishly dug for myself by giving Eric too much power far too soon and leaving Jasmine out of my calculations. I had forgotten that it is the prerogative of a lady, and especially of a young lady, to change her mind. If I am too impatient with myself for my mistakes I must remind myself that the transition from one generation to the next is the most dangerous of any in the life of a family business. That is particularly true when more than one family member has a position of power. It would have been a difficult time, whatever I had done.

Jasmine's arrival causes a family crisis; we form Land Combustion.

Once Jasmine had arrived in the business I soon knew that the days of amicable co-operation between Eric and myself were numbered. I therefore started to think of possible ways of splitting the business between the two sides of the family. Eric had his hands on the main levers of power in the management structure and strongly favoured leaving things as they were which appeared to give him the whip hand.

My first approach was to hive off Land Combustion as a separate company. This would have several important advantages. An important one was that it would give me a power base and if the business was a big success it might open the way for Eric and me to split the business between us. But I had to find a way to persuade Eric to agree to it. It is difficult to remember those days of iniquitously high taxes in the U.K. which distorted business decisions. It was a time of clever and convoluted business schemes designed to circumvent laws that strangled initiative and bled off profits into the Treasury. I knew that Eric was concerned, as we all were at that time, about the devastation of small businesses by high death duties. I produced a gem of a scheme that allowed our combustion business to be split off as a separate company. This company would be owned by the sons and daughters of the family directors (Roy Barber included) who would hold all the shares but very little of the working capital. The large bulk of the finance for the new company would be provided by loans from Land Pyrometers. All future profits would belong to the new generation of the family.

Apart from the tax avoidance scheme, my proposal had the more important objective of training a new generation of managers. I would be Managing Director of the new company and Jasmine and Dave Coe could manage sections of the business and get experience in managing something. At the same time it would keep me out of Eric's way.

Now neither Eric nor I was the largest shareholder in the business. I needed the support of ICFC who own 44.3% of our business. They now call themselves 3i and are the largest British investment house specializing in small private companies. Not surprisingly Eric opposed my plan, which put Jasmine into the seat next to the driver, but ICFC were more supportive. Peter Folkman, who was then in charge of their Sheffield office, invited Jasmine, Eric and me to have lunch at their office. We were joined by Alan Martin who had known us since we first had dealings with them and was by then a regional director of ICFC. Over lunch Eric had an opportunity to put his views to the ICFC people and expressed his opposition. Alan was most supportive of my plan and in the end he finished by suggesting that Eric might benefit from a long cruise round the world. So the plan went through.

We had run out of space on the Dronfield site, so once again Audrey and I went out, as we had done 25 years earlier, looking for a convenient plot of land for a new factory. We found what we wanted some five miles away at Sheepbridge and there we built a small factory on a large plot of land giving us plenty of room for growth. In August 1980 Land Combustion Ltd was formed and we moved in.

Fig. 7.2 The Land Combustion factory at Sheepbridge

Dave Coe leaves Land Combustion and Jasmine becomes Managing Director

We shall see in Chapter 9 that Land Combustion has had a bumpy ride ever since the day that it was formed. But the wave that threatened to sink the ship was Dave Coe's decision at Xmas 1981 to leave and establish his own business. When Dave realized that Jasmine was going to stay in the business and make it a career he decided that his prospects at Lands were too limited for his ambitions. He preferred to be his own boss and why not? Not surprisingly, he started a business in competition with Land Combustion; that was the business that he knew. Steve Wisker and a few others decided to join Dave and we began to wonder if the Combustion business would disintegrate. I called an emergency meeting during the Christmas holiday period. Eric had to concede that the only option was to make Jasmine Managing Director of Land Combustion and show what she could do. There were many occasions during the months that followed when I needed to remind her how much she was learning from being in charge in a period of dire emergency. In the end the best of our people stayed with us and our little business survived. But any hope of solving the family problems through great success in Land Combustion vanished and I had to think of a better idea.

Hard times at Land Pyrometers in the early eighties.

During the first years of the Thatcher administration the whole of British industry was plunged into a miserable state of depression. As steel production declined sharply the sales of liquid steel thermocouples and sampling probes declined too. As the exchange rate of the pound rose to dizzy heights it became increasingly difficult to export and foreign companies found it all too easy to compete in the British market. Infrared thermometer sales declined but were helped by the timely arrival of orders for pyrometers for aircraft engines from Rolls Royce.

In these hard times Eric had to dismiss a substantial number of people who were no longer needed. He did so carefully and without undue hardship. He was always good at dealing with people. Much more needed to be done in the area of liquid steel thermocouples and sampling devices and I became increasingly concerned that the urgently necessary changes were being neglected. The business was profitable but at prices nearly twice the prices current in Europe and the protective patents on which we had relied were running out.

Then Eric's sales manager Fred Campbell had a heart attack. His contacts with the steel industry were essential to the success of the business. Eric did nothing to replace him with a younger man. Nor did he get ahead with a cost reduction program which I considered essential. I suggested that we needed to split off the thermocouple business from the infrared thermometer business and that he should look after thermocouples. He would not hear of it; if there was a split it must be under his overall management.

In the early spring of 1982 I began to notice something going on in the remoter parts of my mind. It was a strange experience to notice a resolve forming, coming up from the subconscious unbidden, just happening, me watching. I knew that I would regain control of my business. I had no idea how it could be done; it looked impossible but it would be done.

So I began to think and think how it could be achieved without damaging the business. The most damaging thing that can happen to a business is for there to be bitter open conflict at the top. I had to devise a plan that would not bring the conflict out into the open. My ideas went round and round, week after week, and nothing emerged. In the end I decided that someone from outside might be able to see what I could not. I contacted Alan Martin, now retired from ICFC, and asked him if he would come over and talk to me, which he very kindly did.

I devise a plan to buy out my cousin Eric Land and reorganize the business

Alan had a plan. He suggested that we should appoint a strong outside Chairman who would be "my man" and would see to it that good decisions were made. He even found a man who would be prepared to take on the job and if Eric was not prepared to accept the position, the Chairman could tell him to go. This was an option that I had never seriously considered, believing it was impossible. But just at this time the new 1982 finance act introduced the possibility, new in British company law, that a company could buy its own shares. Alan's comment and the change in the law gave me the idea that I had been looking for. I could use the company's money to buy Eric's shares. It was a grim thought, but a good one.

First I would need the backing of ICFC and I was not at all sure that I would get it. Their policy, I knew, was to back the family member in charge and that, I reasoned, might now be Eric. My doubts were greater because Peter Folkman, who had been in charge of the Sheffield office of ICFC, had moved to Manchester and a new man, Paul Gilmartin, had arrived. I hardly knew him. How would he view this old buffer who wanted to tip up the apple-cart? So I went to talk to Paul with some trepidation.

I need not have worried. Paul explained that each of the businesses in which they had an investment had a file in which the capabilities of the people in the business were assessed and recorded by successive managers. Paul listened to me and then said "In our judgement Land Pyrometers is Tom Land; whatever you want to do will have our backing". I could have sung and danced for joy. What a relief!

Now I had to plan exactly what I intended to do. I had to confide in our Bank Manager because we would need to seek loans from them or from ICFC and this would need Bank approval. Fortunately the business was in a strong financial position and the Bank raised no objections. Then I had to sit down with John Grosse at our accountants John Watson Sons and Wheatcroft, and work out a plan of reorganization in which Land Combustion would be brought back into the main business.

We decided to split the business into three operating companies:

Land Pyrometers Ltd

Land Infrared Ltd

Land Combustion Ltd

Their shares would be owned by a new company, Land Instruments International Ltd which would also own the land and buildings both at Dronfield and at Sheepbridge. I decided to put Roy Barber in charge of Land Infrared, a new creation comprising the assets of the Radiation Division of Land Pyrometers and Land Instruments Inc. in America. Tony Duncan would become Managing Director of Land Pyrometers, which would take all the business in thermocouples and spares including the ElectroNite products. Jasmine would remain as Managing Director of Land Combustion. I added the word "International" to the name of the holding company, not for the sake of grandiloquence, but to remind us all that we must be international or we would surely perish. Of course the detailed planning of the new company structure and the steps that we would need to take to bring it into being would take many weeks. It would not be completed until the end of 1982 but we needed to know exactly what we would do on D day when the changes were made. John Grosse was enormously helpful in all this planning.

I also needed to agree with John the value that we should place on the shares that we were to buy from Eric. The Articles of Association of Land Pyrometers and Land Combustion gave me the right to buy the shares. The articles also stipulated that in case of dispute over the price the matter should be decided by the auditors. I took care to establish a price that John Grosse, representing the auditors, would approve. We could not afford to be too generous. We would need to buy not only Eric's shares but also a nearly equal number of shares from ICFC to avoid their stake in the company increasing beyond the 44.3% that they had owned. Equally I wanted to pay a fair price that Eric would not dispute. I wanted it all to be quick, clean and, as far as such an operation can be so, friendly.

I had seen on previous occasions how fragile the morale of a business can be. When people know just a corner of the facts they rapidly fill in the unknown areas with frightening speculation. If a business is to function smoothly the people in it must know everything or nothing at all; I believe that honesty is nearly always the best policy. In this instance it was impossible to be open with everybody, so I moved with the greatest circumspection and only John Grosse, Jasmine and Audrey knew my plans. Over a period of months I thought through every detail, planning with John Grosse, negotiating with ICFC, discussing everything with Audrey and Jasmine, asking over and over again "what if ....?" The strain was so severe that I had to see a heart specialist to confirm that the pain in my chest was no more than a sign of over-stress; all was well.

We form Land Instruments International Ltd and Eric resigns

On 12 July my plans were ready and I asked first Roy Barber then Tony Duncan to come to our home in Grindleford to see me. It was a beautiful warm sunny afternoon and we sat in the garden and I told each of them in turn what I intended to do the next day. They had both been concerned to see the developing serious family disagreement which was threatening the very integrity of the business. Both were delighted by the solution that I had devised and at the roles that they would play in the new structure. Next I invited Fred Campbell, who arrived looking apprehensive and worried. I told him what I was doing and explained that I did not propose to give him more responsibility but less. He would work for Tony Duncan and in view of his health he could choose to retire just as soon as he wished - he was very close to retiring age. All three were sworn to secrecy until I had spoken to Eric.

That was the nice bit. The nasty bit came the next day when I had to tell Eric. I remember saying to him "sit down; what I am going to say to you will be a big shock; I am going to exercise my right to buy your shares". I knew that the news would be a terrible blow to him and I dealt with him as gently as I could. You do not end so long a business association with a cousin in five minutes and we had a lot to discuss and details to fill in for him, but by the next morning he had cleared his desk and he was gone. I hated doing the job but I felt very much better when it was done. Eric got a good price for his shares and a good pension and I had avoided an on-going dispute that would have ruined the business for everyone who worked at Lands. But I was uncomfortably aware that what I had done, however beneficial to the business, was the outcome of a poor decision on my part. I had given him the job of Managing Director too early and without sufficiently exhaustive thought and consultation. Decisions that involve people need to be taken only after long and careful thought.

The next day I spoke to all our people and explained what I had done and what would happen next. I had decided that each of the three Managing Directors must have full control of their respective businesses, with their own production facilities, product development and sales departments. The same machine shop had served the manufacture of both thermocouples and infrared instruments under Eric's management. Now it would be split and it was decided to build a wall across the workshop area to divide the two. This was immediately dubbed the Berlin wall. We engaged a young accountant to do the accounts for Land Infrared and for Land Instruments International; Jasmine and Tony are both qualified accountants so they did their own accounts.

The management structure of Land Instruments International Ltd

In our reorganization we took great care to avoid building any substantial costs into Land Instruments International. Certain functions such as reception and personnel were transferred to it, but no new people were engaged and no extra lines of authority were introduced. Most of the administration of LIIL was done by Land Infrared people.

The new organization rapidly got going and ran extremely smoothly. I had decided that each of the three operating companies would have, as its board of directors, just four people: myself as chairman, the Managing Director of that company, and the two other Managing Directors. This arrangement ensured that each Managing Director would have a keen interest in the success of the other two companies. In addition we asked Jim Swithenbank to stay as a Director of Land Combustion.

The four Managing Directors also formed an executive committee of the Board of Land Instruments International Ltd. We four had a monthly meeting at which we received reports on each company, discussed policy and worked on important matters of detail that needed to be solved in ways acceptable to all three operating companies. Above all these meetings were training sessions. We had Managing Directors who had only limited experience in their jobs and needed all the help that was available, from me and from each other. We knew each other well and I was delighted to find that Jasmine fitted in just as well as Tony and Roy. The atmosphere at these meetings was marvellous; we had known each other for many years and could afford to be perfectly candid without giving offence. There was a lot of laughter and friendly banter as well as serious discussion and sometimes disagreement. We did not decide things by vote. The person responsible had to take the final decision and carry the can if things went wrong.

Fig. 7.3 The Group Executive Committee, October 1986: Gary Plowman, Roy Barber, Tom Land, Jasmine Harfoot, Tony Duncan.

When we formed Land Instruments International Ltd, ICFC had suggested that we should have a Chairman from outside the Land family and Alan Martin had agreed to do the job for us. I was very content to be Deputy Chairman. When I was looking through some old photographs with Tom McDougall I noticed a picture of Alan as Chairman. You will see him in Fig. 7.4 with the Master Cutler, who was presenting us with an award for our inflation accounting system. Alan is second from the left beside Roy Barber.

THE NEXT GENERATION - JASMINE JOINS THE BUSINESS

Fig. 7.4 Alan Martin with the Master Cutler who was presenting us with an award.

Some years earlier I had made my wife Audrey a director of Land Pyrometers Ltd. - and of course Eric's wife also. I had always found Audrey's advice helpful and when she attended Board meetings she became better informed and therefore better able to help. I was also conscious that if I died Audrey would have a large share-holding and I wanted her to have a good understanding of the business. She therefore remained on the Board of Land Instruments International.

The basic ideas of the reorganization were quite simple but their implementation was complex and protracted. We owed a great deal to John Grosse who, as well as being a chartered accountant, also has a degree in law. The record of the detailed transactions occupies most of the first thirty pages of the minute book of Land Instruments International Ltd. But the basic changes, including the purchase of another computer and the construction of a wall dividing the machine shop into two, were rapidly and successfully put in action.

We buy the factory next door.

In the autumn of 1983 we heard that Marples were moving out of their factory next door and that the factory was up for sale. When I looked at it I thought it was a hopeless proposition because there was no room for car parking. But Jasmine had a good idea.

The buildings were in two parts. The old machine shop was essentially a large shed with a corrugated iron roof. A large brick office block had been added since we came to Dronfield. It was built to a good standard with high rooms, very suitable for our purposes. Jasmine proposed that we should simply demolish the big old building and use the area as a car park, leaving us some 4,000 square metres of excellent office, laboratory and manufacturing space. Once it was suggested it was obviously the sensible thing to do.

We were in a period of industrial depression. Did we need the extra space? Could we afford it? What would we do with our factory at Sheepbridge if we moved Land Combustion into the Marples factory? If the recession ended quickly the rapid growth of Land Infrared might start again and we would soon find ourselves short of space.

Would we kick ourselves for not taking this opportunity or find ourselves with a white elephant of a big new building that we did not need, bought with money that we did not have? In September 1984 we made an offer of £250,000 which was received by Marples with very little enthusiasm and we waited to see if a better offer emerged. Fortunately for us none did and on 31 January 1985 the purchase was completed for the sum of £275,000.

The demolition cost us nothing but we had to spend another half a million on a new heating system, alterations, partitions and equipment. By the time that we had finished the car park and planted some shrubs to make the place look good we had added a new extension at a bargain price. Land Combustion moved back to Dronfield and we were able to let the Sheepbridge factory on a short lease with a view to selling it when the market recovered. The sales of Land Instruments International increased from £8.4 million to £16.6 million between 1984 and 1989, with just a little help from inflation. We were more than glad to have the extra space and the convenience of having everybody on the same site.

Jasmine becomes Managing Director of Land Instruments International

In 1985 I began to bring my three daughters more closely into the direction of the business. On 13 May in that year my daughters Celia and Dafila were appointed non-executive directors of Land Instruments International Ltd and on 31 October Jasmine was appointed Joint Managing Director, 'her responsibilities covering finance, the provision of buildings and personnel'. In the middle of 1987 Roy Barber reached the age of 62 and relinquished his position as Managing Director of Land Infrared, moving to an easier life of half time working as he had planned a few years earlier. This is not a bad idea if you have plenty of other interests as Roy had. Roy's move triggered a landslide of other changes: Tony Duncan took over Roy's job in Infrared, Gary Plowman became Managing Director of Land Pyrometers and other changes followed at lower levels.

THE NEXT GENERATION - JASMINE JOINS THE BUSINESS

By that time Jasmine had at last brought Land Combustion back into profit and was able to pass on the management of Land Combustion to Marwood Dingle who had previously been its sales manager. On 20 December 1987 Alan Martin retired as Chairman and became Deputy Chairman whilst I retired as Managing Director and became Chairman. Jasmine became sole Managing Director; the business needed a younger person in charge and I was very relieved to leave it in such capable hands. Thus after serving a tough apprenticeship a member of our fifth generation took charge of the family business with new people learning new jobs under her supervision.

In the next three chapters I shall explain how the three operating companies fared after the grand reorganization in 1983. The three stories are completely different and you will see how important it was to have a different manager to handle each of them without the distraction of coping with the others.

CHAPTER 8
LAND PYROMETERS HAS TO BE SOLD
1983 to 1989

In this chapter I shall sketch in the story of the last few years in the life of Land Pyrometers. The graph in Fig. 8.1 summarises the complete history of this grand little business whose profits allowed us to build the very different businesses that we have today. This is the story of Land Pyrometers after the big reorganization in 1983, while the story of Land Infrared up to 1987 is told in Chapter 9. Land Combustion had been created only three years earlier so I have decided to use Chapter 10 to tell the whole of its tempestuous story as far as 1989 when Ramon Biarnes took control.

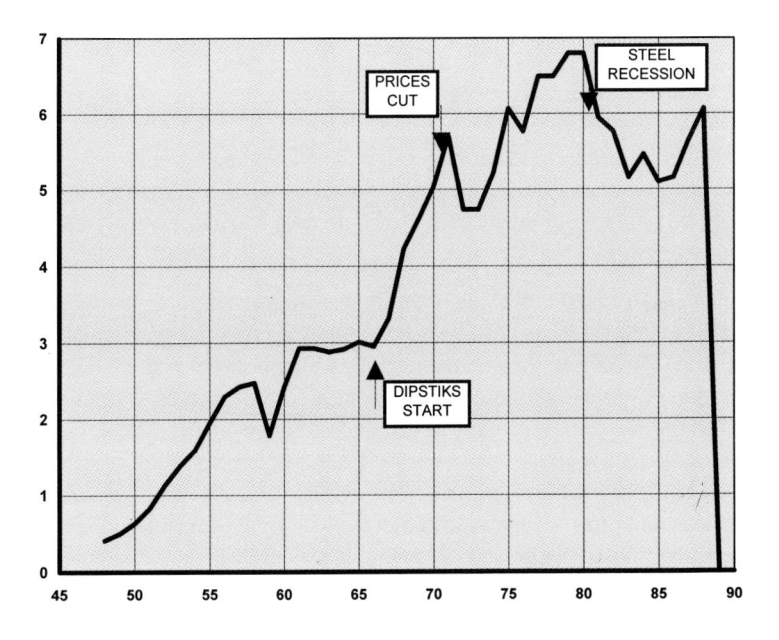

Fig. 8.1 The full history of the sales of Land Pyrometers over 40 years

Tony takes over Land Pyrometers in dangerous times

When Margaret Thatcher's conservative government had come to power in Britain in 1979 it had come on a wave of profound disenchantment with the policies that had taken the country into a dreadful mess. The first result of the new policies had inevitably been to make things even worse. During the year 1980 the output of British manufacturing industry had fallen by nearly 20% and crude steel production fell from 21.5 to 11.3 million tons. It remained at around 15 million tons until 1987. This was bad news for Lands since our business was largely dependent on the steel industry. You can see the dramatic effect on our sales at that time in Fig. 8.1. Fortunately the steel works tended to reduce the size of each load not just the number of heats melted. Eric's careful reduction of staff had enabled us to remain profitable for a year or two. But there was much worse to come.

Our thermocouple business had been the great money-making machine that generated cash to finance the growth of the rest of the business as well as being itself the largest part of the enterprise. We had been in a particularly fortunate position because our business in liquid steel thermocouples was protected by patents held by ElectroNite and by Leeds & Northrup to each of whom we paid 5% royalty. Our only competitor in the British market was Leeds & Northrup themselves, who had a subsidiary company here to sell their recorders and process control equipment. I have explained in Chapter 4 how we succeeded in securing the lion's share of the market at very good profit margins. Now the patents were running out and new and potentially more formidable competitors were at last appearing in the market that had been so comfortable and profitable for so long. Now it was going to be dog eat dog. Luckily we had a bulldog to lead us into the fight.

Tony Duncan had been the obvious candidate to take charge of our thermocouple business. He had shown himself to be an excellent negotiator when we had to agree a price with Rolls Royce for the pyrometer that we designed for their RB199 aircraft engine. He had also handled the discussions with the government's price-fixers most effectively during the period of their prices and incomes policy. When we put in our first computer system it was Tony who chose the system and took it into operation. Now he was ready for a new challenge and we had one for him. Running a small business was a whole new experience and there was plenty for him to learn. I made a point of spending time with him most days, not to tell him what to do but to provide him with someone to talk to about his problems.

Fred Campbell dies; Tony takes control of all functions at Land Pyrometers

Shortly after Tony took charge Fred Campbell, who had become his sales manager, had a second and fatal heart attack. Tony decided that the business was small enough for him to take charge of all aspects of the business himself just as my father had done in his business before the war. There was an urgent need to drive down the cost of production of our main products and that involved negotiating keener prices from our suppliers, going overseas if necessary. This soon showed what savings were available in that area. It was also possible to make substantial savings by introducing further automation in the production process.

When we had first introduced the ElectroNite design of liquid steel thermocouple that we called the Dipstik we had made a point of leaving our competitors a share of the market, so avoiding cut-throat competition. Now that we no longer had patent protection, Tony changed tactics and set out to get every order that he could and soon increased our sales volume substantially. Most of our thermocouple sales went to British Steel who introduced a policy of central buying and Tony was soon negotiating long-term contracts with his usual skill. Prices came down and down but our costs came down as we improved our efficiency and increased our share of the market so Tony succeeded in retaining a respectable profit margin. But it was a hard battle all the way.

We begin to sell the ElectroNite 'Celox' oxygen probe

I explained in Chapter 4 how we failed in our attempt to introduce the Leigh oxygen probe to the steel industry. We failed partly because this Canadian design was not of a sufficiently reliable quality and the excellent results that I had seen in their demonstration in Canada could not be reproduced in European steelworks. More importantly the steel industry was not ready in the nineteen-seventies to use oxygen measurement as a production tool. But Henk Kleyn even then was busy in Holland working with the Royal Dutch steelworks to produce a better disposable probe to measure the dissolved oxygen in liquid steel.

By the time it was ready the steel industry was also ready to use it. When Tony took charge of Land Pyrometers our accounts were beginning to show a category called "Celox". Before long sales of Celox were running at half the value of Dipstiks, making a very significant contribution to the profitability of Land Pyrometers. Unfortunately Celox was imported from ElectroNite in Belgium, not made in Dronfield. At that point our sales of ElectroNite products crept past 50% of the total sales of Land Pyrometers. We had done our best to retain a substantial degree of independence of ElectroNite in our thermocouple business. We were narrowly confined to the small British market and we did not have the resources or the contacts on a world-wide basis that ElectroNite enjoyed and we were increasingly uneasy about our position.

Henk Kleyn organizes a management buy-out of ElectroNite.

We were not the only ones with problems. Tony soon developed friendly relations with Henk Kleyn and learnt that the Littmans had sold ElectroNite to an American conglomerate called Midland Ross. This conglomerate was not well run, either in the way that it nurtured the companies in the group or in the financial success of the whole enterprise. The time came in 1986 when the man in charge realized that he would have to sell the one good company in his group, which was ElectroNite, or lose the whole of his business. Henk had had enough of being part of an American conglomerate. He decided that he would organize a management buy-out and soon he and a group of his top people had committed themselves to investing substantial amounts in the project. He also found financial support from European banks and made an offer to buy ElectroNite which was accepted by Midland Ross. Henk kept us informed by frequent telephone conversations with Tony and of course we took the keenest interest in every detail of the project whose success was of great importance to us.

In these early stages everything went according to Henk's well-conceived plan. But when it came to implementing the promises that had been made the plan began to unravel. First the Chief Executive of Midland Ross refused to implement the agreement that he had made and Henk had to fly to America and bring legal action against him to force him to comply. I thought that Henk would fail but he succeeded. There was a time limit set for completion of the deal, and just before the time ran out the bank on which Henk chiefly depended changed their mind and decided to withdraw their support. I had been watching every detail of the operation sitting with Tony as he talked to Henk on the telephone and receiving daily reports from Tony in whom Henk confided. When Paribas, the French bank concerned, decided to withdraw I suggested that we should seek the help of our friends at ICFC (now called 3i) and Henk was glad to accept my suggestion.

To cut a long and hair-raising story short, 3i succeeded at the very last hours of available time in fixing up a financial package that enabled Henk's plan to succeed. I was delighted that we had been able to make this crucial contribution, both for our own security and to be able to help an old friend. It had been amazing to sit on the sidelines and admire his energy and tenacity. Henk was kind enough to allow us to be part of the buy-out team whose investment was recovered many times over when the company was sold a couple of years later. Our investment of $200,000 made us a net profit of more than £1million which replaced most of the cash that we had had to spend when the company bought out Eric's share of the business.

ElectroNite is sold to Heraeus and we sell Land Pyrometers to them

Henk sold ElectroNite to the famous German family firm of Heraeus with whom he had had friendly business relations for a good many years. They put Henk in charge not just of ElectroNite but of a wider part of the Heraeus organization, including their range of resistance thermometers. One evening at the end of 1988 Tony phoned to say that Henk had been trying to get in touch with me. The news was that Heraeus would like to buy Land Pyrometers. I was very sad but not surprised. I recognized that Land Pyrometers had better prospects as part of the Heraeus organization than as part of Lands. The industrial logic was inescapable and there was no way that we could successfully resist the bid. Jasmine consulted our friends at 3i who agreed that the price that was being offered was a fair one.

So on 31 March 1989 Land Pyrometers, which had funded the development of all our other ventures and which contained so many of our oldest and most faithful friends and employees, became ElectroNite UK Ltd. Gary Plowman, who had by that time succeeded Tony Duncan as Managing Director, went with it. Land Pyrometers had become international by the only available route. I was reminded that when we talk of creating not just a business but a working community, the concept can only be valid within strictly economic boundaries. It is not a club or a church. It is a business and it must obey the logic of business, otherwise it will fail not only as a business but also as a community. But I hated to see them all go.

Fig. 8.2 Signing the agreement to sell Land Pyrometers to ElectroNite, with Henk Kleyn.

CHAPTER 9
LAND INFRARED UNDER ROY BARBER
1974 to 1987

My decision in 1974 to put Roy Barber in charge of our infrared thermometer business turned out to be right. He transformed the little business that I handed over to him into something eight times bigger, better organized and technically ahead of our competitors. When I came to write this chapter I found myself unable to tell the story because I had been at Sheepbridge starting up Land Combustion during most of the time. I therefore asked Roy to write down his recollections of those momentous years. I have quoted extensively from his account and I am most grateful to him for the hard work that he put into its preparation.

It was a great achievement to steer the business as it grew by a factor of eight in not much more than a decade. There were great opportunities but there was also so much new to learn. Roy was not just helping an established business to grow, he was creating a business of a kind quite unlike anything that we had seen before. We were lucky to have in the thermocouple business a source of finance on which to call when the growth of Infrared outstripped its profitability.

The thermocouple business had grown not only by selling more of the same things but also by adding new families of products one after another. The growth of the Infrared business followed a similar course. Every new product line provides a new story with its disappointments and its triumphs.

The Rolls Royce Saga

The first big job that Roy had tackled on his own was the development of a pyrometer to measure the temperature of the turbine blades in a jet engine. It was on that job that he learnt to manage a project. Although it came to fruition in the seventies, the project began right back in 1961 when we had a visit from Tony Neaverson, who was an instrument engineer with Rolls Royce at Derby. They wanted to try measuring the temperature of the turbine blades of the Tyne engine with a radiation pyrometer.

They knew that they could increase the thrust of the engine by 1% for every 10 degrees increase in temperature of the gases streaming through the turbines. They measured the gas temperatures with thermocouples, but they could only estimate the temperature of the blades. If the blades overheated the engine would be destroyed and the aircraft with it. So they had to play safe and put up with reduced engine performance. This is

Roy's account of this marathon project.

'The inquiry came just as we were introducing the early silicon cells into our pyrometers. Once we had persuaded the Rolls Royce engineers of the enormous benefits of using the new 'magical' silicon solar cell, it looked easy. The specification was a doddle - so we thought. We soon found the error of that assumption, and even today we are still making improvements. The optical and temperature range specifications were indeed a doddle, but we were not used to having to run the detector up to 250ºC with ferocious levels of vibration and dirt on the lens.

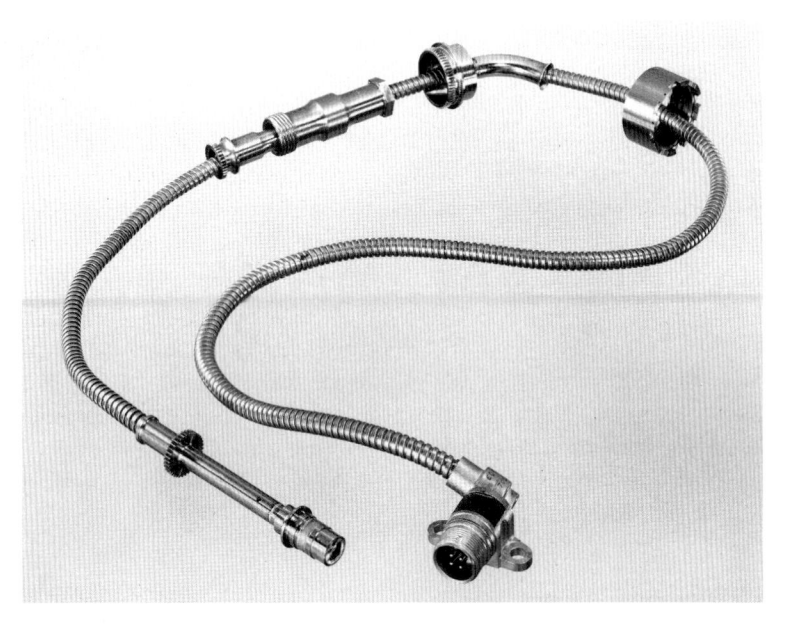

Fig. 9.1 Turbine Blade Pyrometer.

'Two big break-throughs came. First Ferranti started making cells in the new encapsulated format that had been developed for transistors. Later, optical light guides that could stand the harsh environment became available, and we were able to move the detector to a rather safer position. We thought that we had a viable product a year or so later, but Mr. Howard, the Chief Engineer of the Tyne engine, attended a meeting and announced that "He didn't like it—we should start again".

'Shortly after this, we were told that they had decided that we must switch our attention to the engines being designed for the Concorde, where there was a more urgent need for the technique. So! we moved to the Rolls Royce plant at Filton near Bristol and met a whole new set of engineers and designers (except for Mr. Howard, who had just changed jobs). Several of us learned the route to Filton very well. On one famous occasion, Mike Rucklidge got it to such a fine art, that he was waiting in the reception when their first engineer arrived for work. On the whole, we found the Bristol team to be very positive in their approach, and the design went well, until the management decided that they had already overspent by an enormous amount, and there would be no more changes to the Concorde.

'However, all was not lost, we once again changed our attention, this time to the RB199 engines being designed for the multinational Tornado fighter bomber. **At last**, in 1977, we started an 'Aircraft' category in our management accounts, with net sales for the quarter of £3.1k. Eighteen months later this number was £310k, and it has continued to be what Arthur Daley would call "a nice little earner". In addition, we still have a top-supplier rating with Rolls.

'This project has been the best example that I can think of, of the benefit of being a private family business. How many big companies would have supported a project (and its increasingly desperate and embarrassed manager) for that length of time? This time, patience paid. We undoubtedly have a world No 1 status in this field and will, hopefully, build on this with GE and others.'

Other Turbine Applications

The Rolls application started a considerable chain of events. Firstly it created interest with possible competitors. There has always been great rivalry between Rolls Derby and Rolls Bristol; you would often think that they were deadly competitors as indeed they had been before Hawker Siddeley had merged with Rolls. When we moved to Bristol, some of the Derby engineers were not well pleased, so they invited Smiths Instruments (who were already established aircraft instrument suppliers) to develop a pyrometer for them. In addition, one or two American companies became involved. Roy's reaction to the developing interest of the aero-engine industry illustrates the energy and enthusiasm that he brought to the task.

'We realized how little we knew of the military market, which worked in (to us) a very strange way; who you knew was as important as what you were selling. We decided to reach an agreement with someone who knew their way around the Ministry of Defence. Negretti & Zambra were well known to us for their industrial instruments, but they also had an aircraft instrument division. They seemed a good choice, particularly as they had an agreement with an American associate. For a number of years we worked together in the U.K. and with their associates in America. I remember one particular US visit when I'm sure that we out-did the most adventurous American tourist around Europe. In the one week, we visited seven companies and one airforce base, covering Florida in the SE, Connecticut and NY State in the NE, Wright air force base and Cincinnati in Central U.S.A., and two plants in California, one of which was manufacturing the main engines for the Space Shuttle. I had gone to great pains to pack everything in a small case that could be carried onto a plane, in order to save time at the terminals. When I arrived at JFK airport I was met by the American representative of Negretti carrying two large cases.

'In 1977 we had started an Aircraft Section with Peter Kirby, Val Gilday and newcomer Neil Oxley with a few others. We were taking this very seriously. America was obviously the largest potential market, and in 1982 Peter Kirby agreed to move to the US for two years to help the Negretti/Land Consortium to establish some business there. He moved with Judith to Phoenix Arizona (it seemed a good central base), and ran his office from his home, with secretarial help from Judith. He soon realized that there is no such thing as a central base, and he might as well join the rest of the staff at Tullytown. Peter found that many companies were interested in discussing the technique, and even buying experimental models, but it was extremely difficult to persuade them to incorporate a pyrometer on a production engine. Finally in 1982 we had to inform N&Z that we didn't think that we were getting anywhere, and wished to terminate our agreement. They reluctantly agreed.

'Peter's two years were almost as elastic as the one year duration of my initial appointment with Land Pyrometers. He is still there, with broader responsibilities. His work has led to a potentially very exciting product line designed for ground-based turbines, and a contact with GE for a pyrometer on their new GE90 high thrust engine. That is still one of today's problem for the good team of the Dronfield aircraft pyrometer section. I wish them well.'

The Great American Market

Eric was ideally suited to running our thermocouple business which was confined to the British market. He had never had much interest in the infrared business with its high technology, its world vision and its risky, volatile market. So, although he had been involved in setting up our American company, he rather forgot about it when it was up and running. When Roy got to grips with his new responsibilities he found that Land Instruments was a sad and neglected group of people in a potentially fertile environment.

When Roy began his job in 1974 we had a viable Infrared Division with a new American subsidiary, some good products and a surfeit of opportunities. The recurrent problem with our infrared business, particularly in the American Market, has always been to get the correct balance between growth and profit. This is plain to see in the following two graphs which illustrate the great accomplishments of this business and its recurring problems.

INFRARED SALES IN £million OF 1995 VALUE

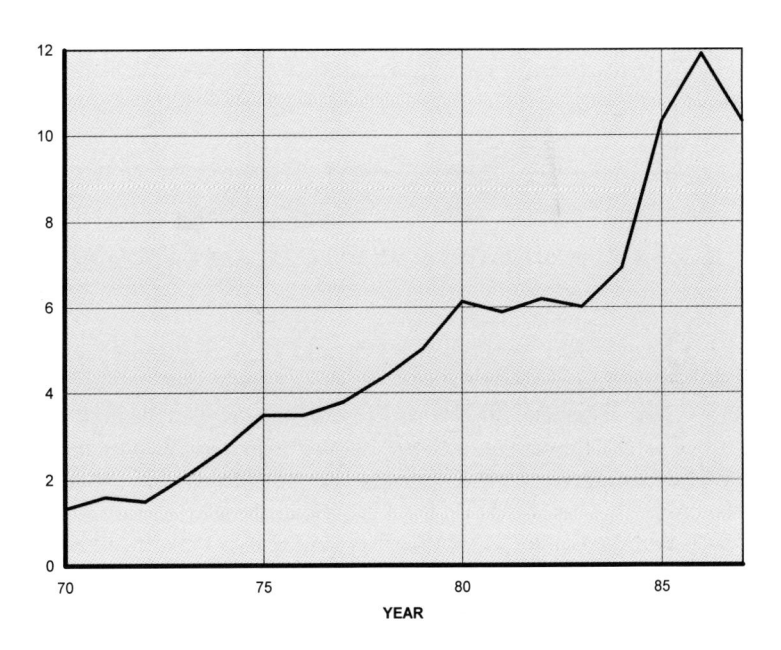

Fig. 9.2 The growth of sales under Roy's management

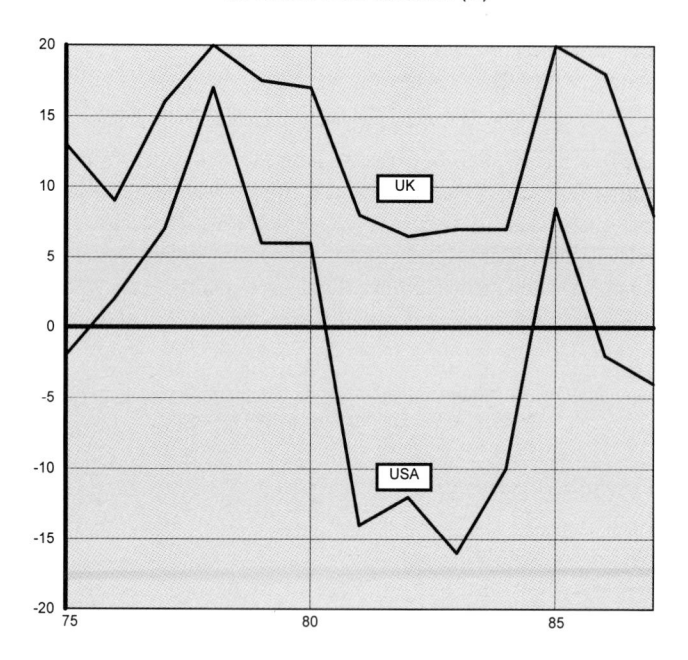

Fig. 9.3 The variation of profit from U.K. and U.S.A. sales

'As we grew', Roy recorded, 'staff and expenses increased to accommodate the growth, and the 'break-even' sales level always seemed to grow at the same rate. Any hiccup or recession dropped the profit to a level that would not fund our growth. We had to be very thankful for the support of the Thermocouple Division and an understanding Board of Directors during these times. Fig. 9.3 highlights the special vulnerability of our American venture. The American market is, at the same time, the most potentially important area for us and the most frustratingly difficult.

'I had first visited America in the days when Don Nielsen ran Atlantic Pyrometers from his home in New Jersey, but by the time that I had any direct responsibility for them, they were well established in the concrete block palace at Tullytown, just north of Philadelphia. Don was nearing retirement. He had overcome his liking for a one man band and there was a small team of workers running a network of Manufacturers' Representatives. This was the normal practice in the States, and is quite necessary in a country of that size. However, as we constantly found out, it is far from an ideal way of deploying the know-how on which our reputation was largely based. Even if the better Reps allowed one of their salesmen to come to Dronfield to be trained they often, quite soon, moved on to other jobs. We were back to square one.

'We were finding an immense difference between being market leader, (as we are in the U.K.) and No 9 (as we later found we were in the States). Although, as Tom reported earlier, we had an excellent technical reputation with a few companies in America, we were largely unknown to the bulk of potential users. Companies such as Ircon and Raytec dominated the market, and we had (and have) to work very hard even to get a fair hearing. *(DAYDREAM, if only we had been able to start a few years earlier!)*

'It was also said, by several Reps, that we did not have the right products for America. This usually meant that they were the type of Rep who didn't like tackling the technically difficult applications. However, they did have a good point, as was seen when the portables were introduced. Now, for the first time, we had a product that was far better than the competitors' and which did not require much application knowledge to sell it. They sold like hot cakes and soon became a disproportionately high percentage of the LII budget. The snag with such a success was that it deflected our attention from the need to solve the main problem and left us vulnerable to the whims of the dollar/yen exchange rate.

'One additional major problem of our lowly status was that it was difficult to attract top class people to the company. In order to improve the quality of staff, and to increase the knowledge base, we had to export people from Dronfield. John Merchant had moved in 1974 and was appointed as Marketing Manager, with Ray Peacock as Engineering Manager. When Don finally retired in 1976 Ray Peacock was made General Manager. Unfortunately this disappointed John, who left in 1979 to work for a competitor and we were again short of application expertise.

'1981/2 saw some drastic changes. It had become apparent that Ray was in the wrong position as General Manager. He would be happier and more effective in his original technical role. Tony Duncan had made his first visit with me to look at the LII accounting methods. Due to a ruptured disc in my spine, I had to ask Tony to go back to persuade Ray that the proposed move was in his best interests, as well as the company's. I was very grateful for his help, as these situations are never pleasant. There was one good spin-off: I realized how good Tony was - despite being an accountant! I thought that we might make something of him one day.

'I persuaded Mike Brown to move to Tullytown as General Manager. He was followed by Norman Fisher, Richard Gagg and others. We now had a better base of knowledge in America, even though some wives did not take to the American way of life and the family then had to return to Dronfield. We continued to grow, albeit not as profitably or as rapidly as we would have wished. In 1984 we opened an office in California, and in 1986 were able to move into a custom built modern factory in an industrial park near Bristol, not too far from Tullytown. The building was also designed to accommodate Land Combustion Inc. who were also outgrowing their previous offices.

Fig. 9.4 Land premises at Bristol.

'Back in 1982 we had organized a Distributors' Conference at the Hallam Tower Hotel in Sheffield. In October 1985 Mike Brown organised our second Distributors' Conference, this time in America, at the interesting venue at Hershey. This is the equivalent of Bourneville, being the private town built by the American chocolate mogul. The conference was a great success, as we were able to launch System 3 (more anon), and get input from nearly all our world-wide distributors. We are learning all the time, but America is still a major challenge. I would love to be able to say that I had cracked it, but I had to leave Tony something worthwhile to do.'

Fig. 9.5 Roy Barber, Shirley Nielson, Meriel Barber and Don Nielson.

Portables

Portable radiation pyrometers had been around for a long time even when I went to work at Jessops in 1939 but they relied on the skill of the operator and would only measure red-hot surfaces. On one of my visits to America Don Nielsen and I were returning to his home on the north side of New York when he decided to call on a young man called Don Michaels who had once worked for him. He had set up business in an old house with a few other people. The business was called Mikron and they were starting to make a portable low temperature infrared thermometer. For a few years we imported and sold these instruments. Eventually we decided that we could make something better ourselves. This is Roy's account of what happened next.

> 'We made a technically acceptable product. Just as we were about to launch the product we learned from Ike Sakaguchi at Kawaso that the Japanese camera company Minolta were planning to do the same. They had adapted a photographic exposure meter that they had developed for the NASA moon shot. (There is not much difference between an exposure meter and a radiation thermometer).

> 'Ike arranged for me to visit the Minolta headquarters in Osaka. When I saw their model and learned of their specification (which severely dented my pride) I was delighted to come away with an agreement that enabled us to have the exclusive sales rights for everywhere other than the Far

East. The whole meeting only lasted half a day. From what I now know about the Japanese decision making methods, I can only assume that they had made the decision to go with Land before our meeting. Whatever the reason, we have had repeated cause to be pleased with the outcome. Despite fears that we might be encouraging a potentially serious competitor, we have had nothing but successful co-operation with Minolta and there is a high level of mutual respect.

'The earlier models proved to be world beaters, and these have been improved and added to over the years. Although we have passed the peak sales for these thermometers and there are now good competitors, they still play a very significant part in our product portfolio. I know that Ircon were jealous of our association with Minolta, and I would like to acknowledge my personal respect for Minolta's design and manufacturing skills'.

Fig. 9.6 Our extensive range of portables.

Thermal Imagers

Although these may be classed as another 'portable', they are a different story. Thermal Imagers had been available for some time before they started to be used in industrial environments. They had been developed for military applications, e.g. to see enemy soldiers and tanks at night. They were also well established for medical diagnostics.

They create a visual image of the infrared radiation emitted by all objects. We had realized that they were a logical extension to our product range, so we were interested when we heard of a small group of specialists who were setting up on their own. Geoff Beynon remembers ringing them up in England when he was visiting Mike Brown in America. Here is Roy's account of what followed.

>'The group was headed by Mike Seggery (an electronics and microprocessor specialist), Dave Freeman (an optical design specialist), Sam Davidson (marketing), and Mike Millard (a mechanical designer). They had left a company called Laser Gauge, believing they were getting nowhere in their plans to move from funded military products to industrial imagers. They had formed a company called Eagle, and had improved the design of a portable instrument. They were looking for a company that would support their venture, and perhaps market the product.
>
>'We thought about this long and hard, finally deciding that we should work with them only if we could take control of Eagle. They, in turn, had to think very hard as to whether they would sacrifice their new found independence. Finally a compromise was reached in which they kept their independence but Land had an exclusive licence to manufacture and sell mutually agreed products. Both parties were taking considerable risks. Ultimately, a few years and many thousands of pounds later, both sides began to think that we might have made the right decision. I certainly had some sleepless nights and, once again, was thankful for an understanding Board.
>
>'There was not a lot that a marketing man could do, during the development stages, so Sam became bored and asked to be bought out. This was arranged with money advanced by Land, against any future royalties that would some day be due to Eagle. Adrian Butterworth later decided that he would like to transfer to Dronfield. Apart from these changes, the program has gone ahead as planned.
>
>'Once again, Minolta played a significant part in the design stage. They had originally been thinking of designing their own imager, but when we approached them with our prototype model they agreed on a joint venture. Minolta were to update the design, manufacture the product and sell it in their area. They made a beautiful job of the design, as you can see from the photograph (Fig. 9.7).
>
>'However, in 1987, we finally realized that their manufacturing costs were too high to make the product saleable. The agreement was re-negotiated and the manufacturing was to be done at Dronfield. (What an about-turn from the 50's and 60's, when everything made in Japan was

half the U.K. manufacturing cost!). I have been delighted with the progress of his project since Tony and John Dixon took over, and even more exciting developments are under way. Once again, it looks as if perseverance has paid off.'

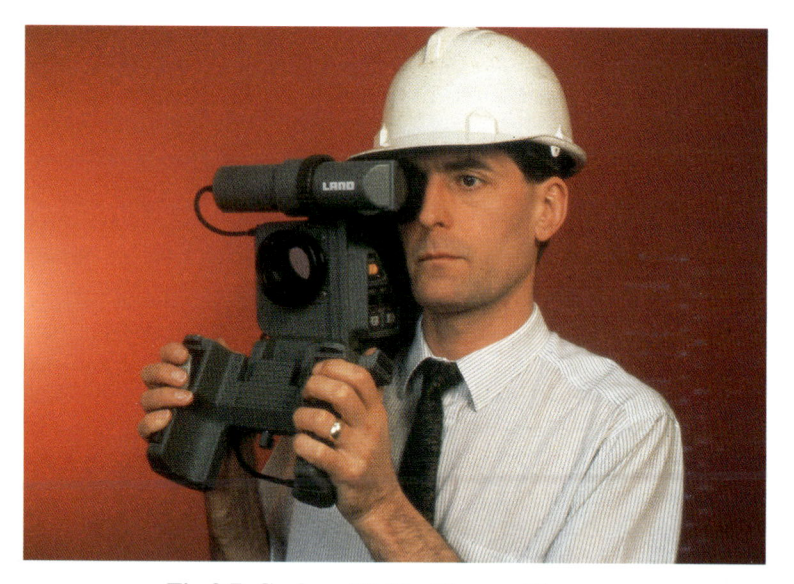

Fig 9.7 Cyclops TI 35+ Thermal Imager.

Marketing

Marketing is a marvellous word with 101 interpretations. It can mean the person who stops you in the street, to ask if you buy Persil. It can be a department that dictates sales policies, or a sub-section of the sales department etc. - etc. Roy knew that it was important, because he was repeatedly told that it was the core of Ircon's success, and that we should ask our customers before we developed a new product. Roy explained that it was a long time before he felt that he understood its place in our future.

> 'It is undoubtedly true that we were a technically led company. This is the essential basis of any young, technically innovative company and, I believe very strongly, the major reason for our position in the market. However, it is equally true that we were so busy following up new product opportunities that we were not making the most of those that we already had. We were not optimising our opportunities.

> 'In 1983 I received an invitation through the post to attend a three day seminar on marketing at the Cranfield School of Management. This sounded too good to miss, it was FREE. The presentation was a complete eye-opener. I realized that the whole basis of marketing is KNOWLEDGE.

Know yourselves, your products and your customers, both present and potential. Cranfield were obviously good at their job, because they persuaded me to use their services to help us to prepare a Marketing Audit, followed by a Marketing Plan.

'They offered the services of one of their consultants called Richard Yallop. I was frequently reminded of the wry definition of a consultant, as a man who borrows your watch to tell you the time. Certainly, by the time that the 300 page Audit document was produced several members of the staff, particularly Marwood Dingle and Mike Brown, were very glad it was over. Richard forced us to answer the difficult questions that we would be tempted to duck. At the end we knew more about our position and our future than I would have believed possible.

'We had produced a SWOT analysis, and therefore knew our Strengths, Weaknesses, Opportunities and Threats. We knew the market potential in most areas of the world and our share of that potential. We also knew our ranking position in each market, and the name and ranking of all competitors. This information, which is periodically updated, enabled us to produce a plan for the future and a company objective.

'Another aspect of marketing is to study your product mix (or product portfolio, to give it its Sunday name). Products are split, in the Boston Matrix, into four categories. Some which are mature are being "milked" to produce profits (Cash Cows). Those that are going nowhere should probably be axed (Dogs). Newer ones with a bright future are Stars and there is a fourth category that may be called problem children because you are not really sure where they are going. We certainly had some of each of these categories, and we needed to do some pruning.

'The study didn't change my mind about the place of customer input in deciding on what a product should look like. I still believe that it is better first to learn of the customers' problem(s). If you believe that you may be able to produce a solution that should be saleable make a prototype and THEN ask for his input. It is much easier to comment constructively when you have a product to act as a starting point. In addition you will have a better idea of what can and what cannot be done. Geoff says that this should be carved in stone somewhere.

'Perhaps my rather jaundiced views on this are influenced by the outcome of our first really serious attempt to do a market study on a proposed new product line. This was for System 3 (of which more later). We knew that we were not producing a revolutionary new product and that, in some aspects, this would have to be a "me-too". Particularly in America, our sales staff were keen that we should produce something that was competitive with Ircon, Mikron and others.

'So, on one of my visits to Tullytown, I spent the best part of three days, mainly with Mike Brown, studying the mass of competitor literature that Mike had assembled. (The magnitude of this can be judged from the fact that, one evening when I arrived back at my hotel, I unpacked my bag and found that I had picked up the Philadelphia phone book with the other leaflets, and I'd never noticed). The outcome of this marketing study was that we produced five processor models. They ranged from Landmark 1, which was to compete with a newly introduced Ircon product, through to the state of (our) art Landmarks 4 and 5. In retrospect this was probably the correct decision, as it enabled our salesmen to offer a product that was as cheap as most competitors, but it is interesting to note that the cheaper models hardly sold at all. We would probably have managed quite well if we had left it to the technical staff.

'I know that we now have a much better balance between the inputs from the various departments (including Production at last). We are learning from experience and finding that you can't learn everything about marketing from a book, or even from a course, but they help.'

Microprocessors and System 3

So far, I have only mentioned the successful projects, but we had our fair share of unsuccessful ones. One of them had a happy ending. I have described my early dream of becoming a broad based 'Instrument Company'. Roy fell for the same temptation when Levy Venn, our Belgian distributor, described to him a new microprocessor based process controller that one of his brothers had developed. This is Roy's account of this adventure.

'The Venn brothers had a bright idea, but they didn't have the production or market base they needed to launch the product. We were too naive to realize that we didn't either, so we agreed to co-operate with them. The instrument was designed to be used in process plants, which, at that time, used many individual controllers for the different functions that needed to be controlled. Using the new digital technology of microprocessors, the Venns had created a single unit that could take 64 inputs and use these to control up to 24 different functions. In principle this was very exciting, and Keith Moore and Andy Mellor spent many weeks in Belgium learning all about the equipment.

'Our downfall was that we didn't have the experience, or the customer contacts, needed to introduce such a new concept to the process control users. Other companies did, and, before we could make the breakthrough, they had beaten us to the punch. Their instruments were more user friendly, as they were already familiar with the needs of the industry. We had to admit defeat.

'The happy ending was that the experience and knowledge that Keith and Andy had acquired in Belgium, enabled us to develop a new range of thermometers and processors to supersede System 2. With great inspiration, we called it System 3. Andy has estimated that the experience with the controller saved two years on the development of System 3, as well as improving its quality. We were, at last, able to take advantage of a Trademark name that had been registered many years previously, when we were thinking of making recorders, namely Landmark.'

The pictures below show the Landmark processors and a System 3 Thermometer. the use of microprocessors, and digital techniques, had enabled us, once again, to make a product that led the market in accuracy and performance.

Fig. 9.8 System 3 showing the thermometer and the signal processing unit.

'We had one disappointment when we launched System 3. It was amazing how long some users wished to stay with System 2. This was particularly true in Japan. It was several years before we were able to convert them to System 3. Their steel plants are apparently great believers in the principle "Better the Devil you know".'

Organization and Staff

These two factors are inter-linked and there always has to be a degree of compromise between the optimum organization and the optimum use of available talent. This was never more true than in our many attempts to solve a recurring problem in the development, production engineering and production chain. At one end we always seemed to fall behind schedule due to unforeseen problems in development. At the other, problems were arising in the finished product, apparently due to lack of communication between the development and production areas.

Many of these problems have now been solved (or largely reduced) by the implementation of the disciplines of BS 5750 and the later ISO9001. At the time we had to try other methods. Roy was very interested in Minolta's solution to the problem and commented as follows.

> 'Minolta ensured that at least one of their technicians from each project, moved between departments when the product moved on. In this way they avoided creating a knowledge gap at each transfer stage. At the end of the cycle the technician joined a new development team. Unfortunately we didn't appear to be large enough to implement this scheme, so we had to compromise. Probably the most successful idea was the creation in 1981 of the NDA (New Developments & Applications) section. This left Keith Moore and his team in charge of the proper production engineering of established product ranges, and their offspring. Keith had a great eye for detail, and was never satisfied until he had got everything to his liking.

> 'The NDA department was headed by Geoff Beynon. Geoff had joined Lands in 1977 from the unlikely background of the Astrophysics Department of Oxford University. After working in the Aircraft Section for about two years he decided that he wasn't sure that he liked the frozen north, and resigned to join Harwell. Fortunately for us he quickly realized that he didn't get any job satisfaction at Harwell, so he re-joined Land a year later. With his small team he was exiled to a Terrapin hut in the yard. (We were getting short of space). This isolation allowed him to try out ideas that later proved to be key elements for many of our present day products. Amongst these were very high speed amplifiers, improved fast thermopiles and new linearizing circuits which led to thermometers for ground based turbines, scanning thermometers and elements that later led to System 4. There was considerable rivalry between the two new sections, but the benefits far outweighed any such disadvantages.'

Russia and Svet

One of our present-day range of products had a fairly bizarre origin in Russia. Roy had met Professor Svet at a number of international committee meetings. He was a member of the Academy of Sciences, and headed a team of temperature specialists at a research establishment in Moscow. We were contacted by his organization and asked if we would like to reach an agreement to commercialise one of the Professor's inventions. The accompanying literature suggested that he had found a magic way of making a radiation thermometer that was independent of the surface being viewed. This was like saying that they had finally found the Philosopher's Stone that turned base metals into gold. We knew it was impossible. But Svet was not a fool, so we needed to find out more. This is Roy's account of his visit to Moscow.

'Keith Moore and I set out for Moscow with draft co-operation and secrecy documents, and the technical papers. When we landed we still did not understand how this idea worked. We were shown the prototype in the laboratory, where it measured accurately the temperature of a tungsten filament lamp and a black body lamp. This was impressive, but even after Svet's description we were none the wiser. He had (and still has) a remarkable ability to confuse us with mathematics, and to run out of English if we asked awkward questions.

'We next visited a large iron works in the Ukraine. All the way on the plane they insisted that we went line-by-line over the Protocol of our agreement. When we arrived we saw the instrument measuring the temperature of the liquid iron stream from an enormous blast furnace. (This one furnace produced more iron than the whole output of the British steel industry). We knew how difficult this measurement is, particularly on this scale. We were impressed, but we still didn't know how it worked.

'What we did find out was that The Soviet Union was not a single nation. The differences between the Muscovites and the Ukrainians was remarkable. The Muscovites were dour and apparently lacking humour, while the Ukrainians said "Take no notice of them, let's have some fun". (That involved going nude-dipping in their outdoor recreation club pool and playing Russian billiards with large aluminium balls).

'On the way home on the plane there was almost a cry of "Eureka". The penny had finally dropped. It was not the Philosopher's Stone, but it was a clever way of taking advantage of practical relationships that exist between the properties of some surfaces at two or more wavelengths. We realized that Svet needed our help mainly to get access to the microprocessors that were not available in Russia. We also realized later that Svet did not have the degree of experience that he would have us believe. So, despite many visits both ways, we were not able to use his instruments.'

I have noticed on several occasions that once you know that someone else has solved a problem it becomes more likely that you will solve it yourself. When Roy told me that he and Keith had at last spotted what Svet was talking about I decided to take another look at the mathematics of two-colour pyrometers. After chasing the equations round two or three sheets of paper it dawned on me how it all worked. What is more I could see how to design the signal processor and how to calibrate the instrument. I showed the results to Roy and Geoff Beynon and we took out a patent. Whether we use the same method as Svet I do not know. But when they had time to try out my idea Geoff and his colleagues found that it worked. But it requires very great precision in design and calibration.

Visiting China

It did not take a marketing genius to realize that China is an enormous potential market. So, in 1976 we took advantage of a Department of Trade sponsored exhibition in Peking (local name Beijing). Martin Johnston took a Combustion stand, and Roy took Infrared products. They stayed in the Friendship Hotel which had been built by the Russians to accommodate their technical advisers. This was rather Spartan, but, at that time, there was only one quality hotel in the city. This is Roy's account of the visit and its outcome.

> 'We learned that the exhibition was by invitation only. There were lots of visitors, but it was extremely difficult to tell who were interested in our products, and who were having a day out. There was obvious reluctance to talk freely to us, even by our translators and technical 'advisors'. It was heavy going. This was not helped by the fact that some of the 'old hands' amongst the other exhibitors kept being asked to meetings at various government offices. This first visit was an initiation test. We did however receive orders for quite a few of the demonstration instruments, so it wasn't a total loss.
>
> 'We must have passed the test as we were asked back in 1978 to give lectures on our products. These were held in the Friendship Hotel, which comprised five tower blocks, interconnected by underground tunnels. 'One of my major surprises occurred in one of the tunnels as I was trying to find my way to the lecture room. An elderly gentleman was shuffling along with a very large Thermos flask in each hand. He stopped and asked me in immaculate Oxford English "Can I be of any assistance to you?" This highly educated man had been one of the victims of the "Cultural Revolution". We learned much more about the devastating

effect of this Anti-Cultural period when all people perceived to be elitist were sent off to the communal farms. Children were told to ridicule their teachers. The overall effect was to take a whole slice out of the educated population. Well educated people were either quite old or quite young.

'The lecture had more in common with the Spanish Inquisition than a technical presentation. After I had been asked "could I come back the next day as they had a few more questions?" I think that the lecture lasted about 9 hours. Several notable changes had taken place since our first visit. Dancing with foreigners was allowed, but more spectacularly there was no more spitting allowed. Beijing has almost zero humidity for much of the year, and sore throats were inevitable. During our first visit, the streets were extremely insanitary. We were told that the law forbidding spitting was 'enforced' by ridicule. All school children had been told to point to anyone that they saw breaking the law. I still find it hard to believe how effective this was. China is an extremely authoritarian country.'

'The third visit was again by invitation. This time we were to negotiate a know-how agreement with a government advisory organization in Shanghai and an instrument manufacturing company in the southern province of Yunnan. I believe that we were the first western visitors to the factory near Kunming, and we were the source of much amusement to the children. My main recollection was one of extreme cold. Apparently no heating was allowed in offices until Nov. 12th. We all sat during the negotiations, with top coats and gloves, clutching the latest cup of tea for extra warmth. I became very attached to Chinese tea. This was the reason why a great number of people were seen carrying the two litre Thermos flasks. You placed about six or seven of the large green tea leaves in the bottom of your cup, and added water. When the cup was empty you just filled it with water again. The leaves lasted for several cups. I was told that, the better the quality of the tea, the lower the temperature of the water. Thermos water was amply hot.

'The agreement was signed and visits were exchanged with technical staff. Some of the stories from these visits could be the basis of another book. I know that Jim Lycett and Vic Cox still have memories of Yunnan, and my wife certainly remembers the time their first delegation came to dinner. We still don't know if this cloud has a silver lining. They bought many parts to make System 1 thermometers, but there has been very little follow up.'

Fig. 9.9 Delegation of Chinese visitors to Dronfield.

Roy's Summary

Roy concluded his notes with the following paragraph:

'I consider myself very lucky to have worked in a family business like Lands, and would like to thank many of the excellent people with whom I worked. I have never been bored, and have had a great deal of job satisfaction, despite the periodic clangers that I dropped. I hope that many of you who read this will be equally satisfied with their lot, and will contribute to an ever improving company.'

Visiting the foreign Customer

When I had finished writing Roy's contribution it occurred to me that I should conclude with a story by someone involved in the job of getting our thermometers working properly on the customer's plant. I asked Ian Ridley if he had one for me and this is what he produced.

'Christmas 1987 was approaching and the customer was not happy. His new furnace control system was up and running but clearly it was not right. Geoff Beynon said "Ian, here's your plane ticket to Rio. You'd better check your yellow fever vaccination because the steel works is in the jungle". So, with a large case full of test gear off I went.

'Our thermometers were measuring the temperature of steel billets in a reheating furnace feeding a rolling mill producing reinforcing rod. The Chief Engineer, Paulo Roberto Cardozo, quickly escorted me through his wonderfully clean factory to the furnace where the thermometer readings were unbelievably high and a plan for the week was agreed.

'The usual instrument checks showed that the thermometers were within specification. In the soaking zone it was obvious what was wrong. The thermometers were looking, not at the billets, but at a pile of scale that had accumulated at the end of the furnace. In the heating zone the furnace was filled with bright and opaque flames which occasionally degenerated into what can only be described as flame soup. Obviously far too little air was being delivered to the burners. When that had been put right it was clear that we needed a second thermometer to get a proper assessment of the effective temperature of the surfaces surrounding the billets. Since the thermometers in the preheat zone had little hope of producing useful results we decided to use one of those.

'Paulo said "show me where and how we should mount it". As we inspected the furnace he said "we have a spare door, could we mount it on that?". "Sure", I said. Suddenly people appeared. The spare jacket and thermometer were removed from the preheat zone, a hole was cut in the door, the mounting plate installed, the insulation cut and the sight tube was fitted. Water and air pipes appeared like magic and a new cable run was pulled through to the control room. In the space of about four hours the door, complete with fully installed thermometer, was being craned up to the furnace for a quick change-over with no thought of shutting down the furnace. The so-called errors were down to a few tens of degrees and we were into the debate about what is the true temperature.

'The control system from Bloom Engineering was also now in order and their engineer Ron Sustich and I decided it was time to leave. "Not so quick," says Mr. Cardozo, "we have other furnaces.... and by the way, a national strike is starting this afternoon and the airport will soon be shut". This was a cue for a quick exit if ever I heard one. With a VARIG, the Brazilian airline, ticket in my hand we set off, only to hear over the public address

"All VARIG flights grounded indefinitely . . . only flights leaving are PANAM to the U.S.A."... "Sorry sir, we cannot accept your Amex card, the phone lines to the banks have been shut off . . .". Fortunately, at this point Ron Sustich saved my day with a typically American wallet full of credit cards, one of which got me to New York.

'It was later through continuing contact with Mr. Cardozo that I learned that the system was saving a fortune in fuel, giving an estimated installed cost pay-back every 10 weeks and that product quality had markedly improved.

Fortunately, not all visits are as hair-raising as this one; but contact with the customer, his plant and his problems are vital in our business. Such vists are always interesting, often challenging and sometimes totally exhausting. We see a vast variety of industrial processes and try our best to understand how they work. The customer may tell you what he wants and you then decide what is the best solution that you can offer him. You must bear in mind that what he really needs is not necessarily exactly what he tells you that he wants. Working together with somebody is the best way to make friends. In our business we make a lot of good friends in the course of solving our customers' problems.

CHAPTER 10
THE TURBULENT HISTORY OF LAND COMBUSTION
1975 to 1989

The nineteen-eighties saw the sale of Land Pyrometers and the rapid development of Land Infrared to become the main part of the company. The same period also saw the beginning of Land Combustion as an independent business. In Chapter 7 I have touched on some incidents in its early years. It is now time to go back and tell you how we got into this business, how it ran into all sorts of troubles and considerable triumphs.

How we got into combustion instrumentation

It might have been more sensible to go into the combustion instrument business in a well organized way, developing a proper business plan and implementing it in an orderly fashion. But no, we just slipped in by the side door without thinking carefully where the door might be leading. The room that we moved into contained some very interesting stuff and had other doors opening into other fascinating areas. Oh dear, that is not the way businesses are supposed to be founded! But in real life things do not always happen according to the text book.

Land Combustion was, in fact, based on a thoughtful analysis of our business as it existed at the time. We saw ourselves as having skills in the development and sale of instruments that were based on applied physics. We knew how to combine the rugged construction needed in an industrial instrument with careful scientific analysis of the problem in hand. We had particular experience in optical methods and in temperature measurement. We had our eyes open for new industrial opportunities where our particular skills could be brought to bear. We noticed gas temperature measurement and flame detection as interesting areas close to our existing business that we should keep our eyes on.

While I was working at Jessops during the war I had published a couple of papers that applied the mathematical theory of heat transfer to some steelworks problems. The mathematical skills that I developed in writing those two papers led us, rather improbably, into the first of these new areas in the early nineteen-fifties. It all began when Dr. Jackson, who was the head of the British Coal Utilisation Research Association (BCURA), asked us to design a suction pyrometer to measure the temperature of the very hot gases in large combustion chambers. That was the first door that we opened.

The theory of suction pyrometers

I must explain why a special kind of instrument is needed to measure the temperature of gas at high temperatures. If you think about it carefully you will realize that any thermometer measures only the temperature of the thermometer itself. If you want to measure the temperature of a gas with a thermocouple you have to be sure that the thermocouple reaches the same temperature as the gas. But in a boiler the thermocouple is surrounded by much colder surfaces (chiefly the water tubes) and it loses heat to these surfaces by radiation. The temperature of the thermocouple lies somewhere between the gas temperature and the temperature of the surrounding surfaces. Its exact temperature is determined by the fact that it must receive the same amount of heat from the gas as it loses to the surroundings. Heat transfer by radiation is much bigger at high temperatures and this makes the problem much more severe in very hot gases.

We knew how to meet this problem, we were not the first people to tackle it. A number of scientific papers had been published describing thermocouples surrounded by several concentric tubes that act as radiation shields to reduce heat loss from the thermocouple by radiation. The hot gases are sucked past the thermocouple and between the radiation shields at a high velocity to increase the heat transfer by convection. Increasing the gas velocity or the number of concentric shields makes the thermocouple attain a temperature nearer to the temperature of the gas. Such devices are called suction pyrometers or high velocity thermocouples.

This was fine, but how many shields would we need and how fast should we aspirate the hot gases through the shields and past the thermocouple? Nobody had worked out a satisfactory theory so I sat down at my desk and solved the mathematical equations. We wrote a paper with graphs and tables showing for the first time how to design a suction pyrometer for any particular set of conditions. We built pyrometers and Roy Barber took them to a power station and checked the accuracy of our calculations. The paper was published by the Institute of Measurement and Control and Roy Barber and I were awarded a prize for the joint best paper of the year. Dr. Jackson happened to be one of the assessors who judged the papers. We were thermocouple manufacturers, so it did not occur to us that this work was going to draw us into the very different field of combustion instrumentation and gas analysis.

The combustion of coal and other fuels

In the nineteen fifties the British coal Utilisation Research Association were among the most advanced organizations working on the combustion of coal anywhere in the world. Electricity generation stations were among the largest users of coal boilers so the BCURA were particularly interested in the efficient operation of power station boilers. The important question was how to get the greatest amount of heat out of the coal that was burnt.

During the subsequent 40 years, research has broadened out into other aspects of the combustion of coal, oil, gas and other combustible substances. It has been increasingly realized that combustion produces a variety of harmful gases that need to be measured and eliminated if possible. Among the most serious are the oxides of sulphur (from the fuel) and nitrogen (from the air) and also carbon monoxide. As we were drawn into the instrumental control of combustion we became involved first in measurements designed to increase the efficiency with which heat was released from the combustion process to produce high temperature gases. Subsequently we found ourselves drifting further away from our 'home territory' of the physics of temperature and heat into the chemistry of gases, with we were much less familiar.

We begin to manufacture probes for measurements in power station boilers

Our work on suction pyrometers got us accepted at BCURA as colleagues and we published a joint paper with some of their scientists. They were working on a very different type of gas thermometer for power station boilers called a venturi-pneumatic pyrometer. It measures the gas temperature by comparing the density of the hot gas with its density at a much lower, easily measured temperature after being sucked down a long water-cooled tube. We then designed and manufactured venturi-pneumatic pyrometers on a commercial basis. We also made water-cooled pitot tubes to BCURA designs; these allowed us to measure the velocity of the hot gas in the boiler and the direction in which it was flowing. When we designed our new factory at Dronfield we made special provision for handling these huge long water-cooled probes and we built a wind-tunnel to calibrate the pitot tubes.

We found ourselves at the spear-head of the excellent work that was then being done in Britain on gases in large boilers. That was rather fun. When other new instruments came to us from BCURA we were able to turn them into commercial products. So we came to make acid dewpoint meters to measure the sulphuric acid content of flue-gases and the Flo-test to detect blocked boiler tubes. Where were we going? By this time BCURA's work had been taken over by the laboratories of the Central Electricity Generating Board (CEGB). We put two good technical people, Gary Plowman and Marwood Dingle, in charge of this small section which later became the Combustion Division. Gary looked after manufacturing and Marwood was the marketing man. For many years this odd little business rolled along on a small scale, providing specialized instruments for research into combustion in big boilers. Then suddenly in the seventies it sprang to life. We came across a new door with a large sign on it saying ENORMOUS OPPORTUNITY. We just had to peep inside.

Burner control

The 'big opportunity' that turned up was burner control. At first it looked so big and so impressive that we wondered if we would be able to handle it. The idea came from Jim Swithenbank who was then a lecturer (later Professor) in the department of fuel technology at Sheffield University. Jim is no ivory-tower academic, he worked for some years at Rolls Royce. One of his PhD students had studied the infrared radiation emitted by flames. He had come to the conclusion that the most efficient mixture of fuel and air produced the highest intensity of radiation from the flame. This is not surprising since it produces the highest flame temperature. Perhaps the fuel/air ratio could be optimized just by making radiation measurements on the flame. That would be fantastic!

The work was being sponsored by Esso Research - so it had to be respectable. Esso had contributed £2,000 and in 1975 Jim asked if we would like to contribute a further £2,000 to complete the work. We agreed to contribute and decided to make some equipment to test the idea on a commercial boiler and I bought a pile of books on combustion and fuel technology, which I read carefully. I was aware that one should always engage the best people on the projects that offer the biggest opportunities. I therefore persuaded Roy Barber to let me pull out David Coe, who was then Product Development Manager, Mike Bray who was a bright young electronics engineer, Martin Johnston from sales and other lively lads to work on it. Dave Coe persuaded David Johnstone at ICI Winnington to let us try out the idea on an old boiler that had been converted from coal-firing to oil.

The work at Winnington

Dave and his team installed a small radiation thermometer to measure the brightness of the flame and connected it to an electronic box-of-tricks. The first purpose of the electronic circuit was to provide a signal to the control system of the boiler to increase and decrease the richness of the fuel-air mixture by a small amount for short periods of time. The signal from the flame thermometer showed that the flame consequently became alternately hotter and cooler over the same time periods. The second purpose of the electronic circuit was to amplify the signal from the radiation thermometer and to find out whether a higher fuel/air ratio was making the flame temperature higher or lower. The fuel-air ratio was then automatically adjusted to optimize the ratio and maximize the radiation from the flame. Such a device is said to be 'peak seeking'.

It was a dreadful old boiler and our people had to get the existing control systems working properly before we could get anywhere with our gadget but eventually they got it working. Fortunately the management took great care to keep the atomising of the oil in efficient condition. Since Eric, who was now Managing Director, did not view the Combustion Department with much enthusiasm I decided to take it under my wing. I remember visiting Winnington with Dave and some of his team. We would put the boiler on 'automatic burner control' and then nip outside and look up at the stack. The plume of grey smoke would slowly disappear as the fuel-air ratio gradually adjusted to the ideal value. It worked!

We thought that we had a marvellous device and we set out to sell our idea to other boiler users. They were pleased to see us and prepared let us have a go. But it was never as easy as it should have been. We found ourselves spending weeks and months discovering why we were not getting results. Sometimes we were not able to get a clear view of the flame. Sometimes the oil was not being properly atomized. Sometimes the oil and the combustion air were not mixing as well as they should. If only the burners had been better designed and maintained life would have been marvellous!

We had been persuaded to engage a firm of marketing consultants to advise us on marketing our wonder-toy. They showed us the enormous market that it would open up and discussed how to handle the huge potential sales. So we kept trying. By 1980 we had made a few very successful installations, but we realized that in the real world our burner control system was not a commercial proposition. We had strayed too far away from our specialization as physicists into combustion technology, where we were too ignorant. Regretfully, we backed off and got on with other, more promising developments.

The acid dewpoint meter

There was no shortage of opportunities. An acid dewpoint meter can be used to measure the sulphuric acid content of the flue gases in a boiler. Oil and coal both contain sulphur. Some oils and some coals have very little but others contain enough to be a dreadful and expensive nuisance. Most of the sulphur is burnt to form the sulphur dioxide (SO_2) which causes the acid rain that pollutes rivers and lakes. Some is further oxidized to form sulphur trioxide (SO_3) which combines with the water vapour in the waste gases to form sulphuric acid vapour which is highly destructive. If the vapour comes into contact with surfaces cooler than the dewpoint of that vapour the acid condenses. If it condenses on metal surfaces it corrodes the metal rapidly and expensively. If it condenses on soot it produces acid soots that may float down on parked cars and remove patches of paint. Our friends at BCURA had invented an excellent acid dewpoint meter that worked very well. It had been manufactured by another firm who gave it up. We had designed a better one and sold it for a good many years. We now decided to update it using modern electronics and added it to our list of combustion instruments.

It sold quite nicely but in many places it was viewed with some scepticism. This was largely because its operation was not properly understood and two respected scientists had published a paper at the time of its inception which cast serious doubts on the whole idea of an acid dewpoint. I decided that we should try to put the instrument on a proper theoretical foundation as we had done years before with the suction pyrometer. I would have time to do it myself.

Fig. 10.1 Acid Dewpoint Meter.

I work out the theory of the acid dewpoint meter

I have always been at my best and happiest when working as a research physicist. I had a wonderful time browsing through the literature in the Sheffield University Library and learning the theory of mass transfer and its relationship to heat transfer. Reading the old papers and working through the mathematical theory, I soon realized that the critics who had cast such doubts on the method had done some excellent experimental work but had drawn quite the wrong conclusions. Then I read about the problem of fog formation in condensers and realized that the same phenomenon was causing anomalous results in our dewpoint meter. As the theoretical work took shape I found that the experimental results of the critics fitted my theory excellently. I was able to publish a paper that explained the deposition of sulphuric acid and the operation of our dewpoint meter quantitatively and unambiguously. When we distributed reprints of my paper with our literature we had no more sceptics doubting the validity of the measurement.

The inventors of the dewpoint meter had decided that it could not be used for continuous measurements. However, Dave Coe found that an ICI plant in Lancashire was having some success with continuous recording. So we decided to try it and eventually produced a successful continuous dewpoint meter. We then had a unique and useful instrument that could be sold with a minimum of effort and still sells well today.

Measuring carbon monoxide in the waste gases

When we were talking to CEGB about our burner control systems they told us that they were looking for a good carbon monoxide meter. Historically, the air/fuel ratio in boilers had first been controlled from measurements of the CO_2 content of the flue gases - the more CO_2 the better. Next had come the oxygen meter which measured the excess air that was being introduced, heated up and wasted up the stack. Our friends at CEGB explained to us that fuel engineers were becoming convinced that a measurement of the carbon monoxide content of the waste gases would be the most sensitive method of getting the last few percentage points of efficiency out of big boilers. Would we like to have a go at a carbon monoxide meter? An infrared absorption meter seemed the best bet and we had plenty of experience in infrared radiation measurement. This was applied infrared physics and we decided to have a look at it.

Jim Swithenbank gave me a paper written by some Americans who had made an infrared absorption meter which I studied carefully. I came to the conclusion that we might use the new photocells that we were using in our low temperature radiation thermometers. They should be just sufficiently sensitive and would make it possible to simplify the instrument greatly. I have always been a great enthusiast for simplicity. So we got some equipment together and made a simple instrument to check out the fundamentals. We installed cylinders of nitrogen and carbon monoxide in the conference room. The room was big enough to dilute any unexpected leak of the poisonous and odourless carbon monoxide gas. We engaged a young fuel engineer and set him to work measuring the absorption characteristics of various mixtures of CO and nitrogen. From this work we went on to build our first, very simple CO meter.

The cross-correlation flame monitor

Next came the flame monitor. The efficient detection of the flames in a pulverized-coal fired boiler is very necessary to prevent explosions in the huge combustion chamber. But it had always been a baffling problem. When the boiler is cross-fired the flame can be observed only from a point close to the burner. Even then, the observer has to look through a cloud of unburned coal-dust that may occasionally obscure as much as 98% of the light from the flame. The flame is surrounded by other flames that can confuse the interpretation of any signal received by a simple flame detector.

The Central Electricity Research Laboratories at Leatherhead had tackled this problem with great ingenuity. They had used not one optical system but two, side by side, to give binocular vision of the flame. Two lenses formed two images of the flame on two photoelectric cells. The two photocells were a little further apart than the two lenses so that the sight paths crossed at a point inside the furnace where the flame would be found.

All flames flicker. If the flame that is being monitored is lit, both photocells will see almost identical flickers. If the flame has gone out the two photocells will be looking across at different parts of the furnace and will see different patterns of flicker from other flames. The two signals will not 'correlate'. The device was called a 'cross correlation flame monitor'. I went to a power station near Leeds where they had fitted their prototype and saw it working and I went to Leatherhead and talked to the scientist in charge of the project. I thought that CEGB had invented an impressive and effective instrument.

The CEGB decided to have 20 copies of their prototype made to give it a fuller trial and we (among others) were invited to tender for 20 instruments. We studied the design carefully and made a realistic tender but to our regret the contract was placed elsewhere. However we were not dismayed. We realized that it would be no easy matter to set up 60 of these monitors on a big boiler. Each head required careful adjustments with a screwdriver. The wiring from all these devices to a control panel would cost a fortune. I suggested that we should leapfrog the prototype and design something based on the same principle but which would be easier to install and more convenient to use.

By this time we were beginning to use microprocessors in our instruments. We decided boldly to replace the two photocells by two arrays of cells. We then put a microprocessor in the head and programmed it to do all the adjustments automatically. We also put a microprocessor at the control panel that would talk to the microprocessors in the heads down a single cable linked to all the heads.

This was a bold and imaginative design; we made it work due to excellent electronic design by Mike Bray. The heads were far more expensive than anything previously contemplated for flame detectors but CEGB were prepared to give them a trial. We were able to tap into funds available from the Department of Trade and Industry to finance a trial installation at Ferrybridge power station.

Our equipment was designed on the basis of information from CEGB about the maximum temperatures likely to be encountered, which sadly turned out to be wrong. How often that happens to us! We would never have dared to risk putting our electronics into equipment that would run at temperatures up to nearly 100°C. Also there were times when the whole boiler developed intense vibration, which we had not expected. So we had too many failures and the customer lost patience with the project. It was to take 3 years before CEGB began to equip their boilers with our 'Flamescan' systems. By that time it was a formidably tough and sophisticated piece of industrial electronics that generated some very large orders. The big Flamescan orders gave us very profitable quarters but when there were none we did not yet have a sufficient flow of other orders to keep us busy and profitable.

Land Combustion at Sheepbridge

By the time that we had reached this point in our development programme we had split off Land Combustion as a separate company as I have already explained in Chapter 7. I had moved with them down to the new factory that we had built. I was amazed to find what a sense of peace and freedom descended on us when we got to Sheepbridge. We were making a new beginning and it was marvellous. I was Managing Director and Dave Coe was responsible for development and marketing, while Jasmine looked after manufacturing and accounts. In 1981 Jasmine's first-born arrived and Martha was brought down to the office for several months where she slept quietly in her carry cot on the office table. Jasmine's husband Larry then volunteered to give up his job with British Rail and looked after Martha and subsequently also Rona and Anna. He was a wonderful father to them. Later he was to have a sheep farm on the hill-top above Eyam where he could enjoy a happy mixture of farming and child-minding!

Land Combustion Inc.

We decided from the first that we must have our own American company. Once again I turned to my old friend Fred Maltby and once again Fred turned up trumps. He agreed to be a director of Land Combustion Inc. and invested $2000 in shares in the company. He had recently bought the factory next to his own and had space to spare. He provided us with space to work, help in setting up the business and all sorts of useful advice. Fred was most kind.

Dave Coe needed someone to run the American business. Rob Kufta had worked at Land Instruments Inc. and he and Dave had become friendly but Rob had not got on too well with Ray Peacock and had left. Dave asked me would it be all right for him to engage Rob? "Your decision" I said. So Rob was invited and took the job. His first success was with the acid dewpoint meter that had been sold by Land Instruments Inc. Its sales, which had been declining, soon responded to more intensive care and we soon had a small but steady line of business on which to base an American venture.

Successes and failures

As I sat in my new office in Sheepbridge I knew that we had a rickety business held together with sealing wax and string. My choice of combustion control as a new area of business had proved all too productive. We were developing too many new products too fast without any substantial core product to pay the bills. We had moved into a new market with new products, a known recipe for disaster. I hoped that we were clever enough to get this machine off the ground before it fell to pieces.

We had successes. Although the Flamescan system that we installed at the Ferrybridge Power Station had given a lot of trouble, the similar systems that we fitted to power stations in Denmark worked very well and they ordered more. Clearly their conditions were less destructively hot and more like the conditions that we had been led to expect at Ferrybridge.

Fig. 10.2 Flamescan.

Our carbon monoxide meters were very different from anything that had been made before. American designs had been developed from the starting point of a laboratory infrared spectrometer. They were large and elaborate. Ours were developed from industrial infrared thermometers. They were small, simple and very crude, but on the oil-fired boilers where they were first installed they worked well. In America, they were seen by Rosemount who believed, like CEGB, that carbon monoxide measurement in large boilers had a big future. Rosemount came to talk to us about a licence.

When we started to use the carbon monoxide meter on a coal-fired boiler we had a nasty shock. In our ignorance we had not reckoned on the problem of dust. Coal contains a lot of dust that has to be trapped by electrostatic precipitators to prevent it polluting the atmosphere and falling on the surrounding countryside. This dust is dislodged from the precipitator every few hours by rapping the precipitator plates. Clouds of dust then travelled up the flue past our carbon monoxide meters, obscuring the line of sight of the meters and playing havoc with the readings. So we had problems which were not quickly rectified.

We had troubles; but we also had encouraging successes. Dave Coe discussed the Rosemount proposition with me and we decided that we would find it difficult to cover the American market adequately ourselves. Rosemount would acquire this technology from someone, we might as well sell them our know-how and make some money. We signed an agreement under which they bought our know-how and they ordered a substantial batch of instruments from us. As a result Land Combustion made a profit of £250,000 in the financial year to March 1982.

These were the wild pioneering days of Land Combustion when we were exploring new territory that we knew all too little about and in which we were hoping to make a living, maybe strike gold. We did things that nobody had achieved before and made awful mistakes because of our ignorance; the aborigines behind the bushes must have had a few laughs! But I remember calculating at about that time that up to that moment we had learnt a vast amount and financially we had broken even.

Dave Coe leaves to start his own business

However things were soon to get much worse. During the latter half of 1981 Dave Coe, who should have been grappling with the serious problems of Land Combustion was, instead, looking at the possibility of starting a business of his own. I think that it was a nasty shock for him when Jasmine arrived at the works. When she continued to work after Martha was born he must have decided that he no longer had as good a prospect of a top job at Lands. He had talked to me about his doubts about working for Eric, but I did not realize that he was seriously planning to set up his own business. So when at Christmas 1981 I received a letter from him saying he was leaving and what he was doing I was taken aback. I immediately called together Eric, Jasmine, Martin Johnston and Mike Bray during Christmas week to decide what to do. I suggested that Jasmine should take over as Managing Director. Eric agreed grudgingly, saying that he didn't seem to have much option. Martin Johnston became Sales Manager and Mike Bray took over product development.

Jasmine becomes Managing Director of Land Combustion Ltd.

It was not only Dave who left. He took Steve Wisker with him and several others followed. It looked as if Land Combustion was in deep trouble. Dave not only took people with him, of course he also took information. There were tales of him working overtime on the copying machine during the weeks before he left. He also left things in a pretty pickle with the work on the carbon monoxide meter neglected and the explanatory documentation for Rosemount unfinished. I had to roll up my sleeves and get the theory of the instrument worked out and written up myself. As usual things were not as calamitous as they first appeared and most of our best people stayed with us.

Ramon Biarnes takes charge of the American subsidiary.

At quite an early stage Dave Coe had recruited a young Spanish physicist called Ramon Biarnes to sell our combustion control instruments in Spain. As our business in America began to grow Dave had asked Ramon if he would like to move to Philadelphia and work with Rob Kufta and rather to my surprise he had agreed to emigrate with his wife Neus and baby Marta and in due course they became American citizens. After Dave Coe left, Rob Kufta left to join him and in 1982 Ramon took charge of Land Combustion Inc.

The next few years were bleak for Land Combustion and I had to remind Jasmine that she would learn far more in adversity than when times were good. We had to replace Mike Bray as Product Development Manager and we were fortunate to get Peter Webb from British Steel who turned out to be thorough and meticulous. Our problems arose chiefly from our over-optimistic assessment of the market which failed to develop as quickly as we had expected. The measurement of carbon monoxide had been expected by Rosemount as well as by ourselves to grow far faster and become far bigger than it did. Also the power stations in the U.K. were reluctant to put their money down and buy Flamescan even when it had proved to be remarkably reliable under adverse conditions.

By 1987 Jasmine had succeeded in getting Land Combustion back into profit and I decided that it was time for her to take over the management of the Group. We had first to find a successor to take over her job at Land Combustion. Marwood Dingle had spent much of his time in the Combustion section and had always done a good, conscientious job so we decided to let him have a go. Some people, like Roy Barber or Tony Duncan, are obvious choices that you make with confidence. Others are quiet people who may blossom when they are given the opportunity or may not have the vital spark. The trouble is that you can never be sure how a manager will turn out in a top job until you give them the chance. Marwood did a conscientious job but sadly the vital spark was not there and we had to think again.

Ramon starts to run the Combustion business from Philadelphia

Ramon had been doing well in America, and in 1987 we had thought what a pity it was that he could not run the whole business from Philadelphia. At that time it was obviously out of the question. Now in 1989 we were again looking for a manager for Combustion and we had to ask ourselves again whether it was really impossible for Ramon to do the job. By that time he had had more experience and his efforts were showing good results in the US market. So we decided that we had better ask him whether he thought he could run the whole business from his office in Philadelphia. He thought about it and came back and said he thought he could. He was young and bursting with energy, so we crossed our fingers and let him have a go. We quickly found that we had let off a fire cracker in Land Combustion. We had put the business in the hands of someone with energy and drive who knew what he wanted to do. It was a difficult task and it took him time to get things right. A man with all his energy is naturally tempted to take all the decisions himself. He is slowly learning that his job is to train managers to take good decisions themselves, to let them get on without interference and to make sure of getting one job right before undertaking the next. I myself had to learn all these essential lessons. A man with drive and energy finds them dreadfully difficult to learn. But good businesses are not created by pussycats.

Fig. 10.3 Some of Land Combustion's distributors from a recent conference.

CHAPTER 11
LANDS RENEWED

Jasmine takes my place as head of a new management team

The history of Lands that I can recount from personal experience finishes in 1987 when I handed over the job of Managing Director of our little group of companies to Jasmine. One of her early tasks unfortunately had to be to oversee the sale of Land Pyrometers to ElectroNite where it grew and prospered, but no longer as part of Lands. By the end of the nineteen eighties the old Lands that had lasted for forty years had been refashioned. My cousin Eric Land had been bought out. Roy Barber had retired from an executive position. The old team had bowed out and the new team of managers had taken over. I remained as Chairman but the running of the business was firmly in the hands of Jasmine and the Executive Committee.

Fig. 11.1 The Executive Committee in 1997.

It was high time for renewal. I had needed to stay on as Managing Director until Jasmine could safely hand over Land Combustion to someone else. By then I was well into my seventies, which was too old for the good of the Company. Roy had been able to take partial retirement in his early sixties which was wiser, but I had to finish a job that nobody else could finish. I cannot recount the history of the Company in detail in the years that have followed, but I can record briefly what has been accomplished.

In the last eight years since we sold Land Pyrometers the total sales, measured in pounds of constant value, have increased by two thirds from £15 million to £25 million and the financial position is now the strongest that it has been for many years. Jasmine has become the architect of the whole enterprise. She is Chairman of the Executive committee that runs the two Divisions of the business and also its Finance Director. She has the enviable ability to go straight to the simple solution of a problem. She can then persuade you that it is the solution that you thought of yourself.

My job as Company Chairman has not been quite what you might expect and the function of the Board has developed in an interesting way. I introduced Jasmine's two sisters Celia Knighton and Dafila Bourchier as Board members alongside Tony, Ramon and Roy, my wife Audrey and an outside non-executive director, Dr. John Watkinson. Thus I had brought the owners of the business, apart from 3i, into close contact with its management. This is how a family business should be. I was acting as head of the family as much as Chairman of a substantial business.

LAND COMBUSTION IN THE NINETIES

How Land Combustion languished during the early eighties

In the mid seventies we saw the new opportunities in the combustion field as being a wonderful new way to put our infrared knowledge to profitable use. It enabled us to develop the remarkable new flame detector that CEGB had invented into a successful and sophisticated instrument. We had a clever young electronics engineer in Mike Bray who could apply the new microprocessor technology to this flame detector and (eventually) make it work well. We could develop an infrared CO meter that was simpler and cheaper than any in the world and avoid the problems that came with sampling.

But what we had got into was not just an extension to our infrared business at all. We had strayed into a new market of which we had no real experience, and we had jumped into the high-tech end of that market. That was not the way you are suppose to start in a new market. In 1947, when I had started Land Pyrometers, I had taken great care to begin with a resale business and only then moved cautiously into engineering and high technology. In the excitement of new opportunities in combustion control, had I perhaps forgotten what I had known and applied so carefully thirty years before? Perhaps so. But you must remember that, without the high-tech instruments based on infrared technology, we would never have considered the business of combustion instrumentation and there would have been no Land Combustion at all. However, the combustion business languished during the early eighties waiting for a new impetus to get it up and flying.

THINK AMERICA!

We have always found the three thousand miles between Dronfield and Philadelphia to be a big problem for our sales in America. During the mid eighties Jasmine had decided that this needed to be tackled very seriously. She had put a big effort into persuading everybody to recognise the great importance of the American market with the slogan THINK AMERICA! Product development was directed towards products for the U.S.A. market. With Ramon in charge in Philadelphia THINK AMERICA set the American sales alight as will be seen in Fig. 11.2. Between 1985 and 1989 sales in the U.S.A. grew from £280k to £1.05 million.

COMBUSTION SALES FROM UK AND USA IN £million

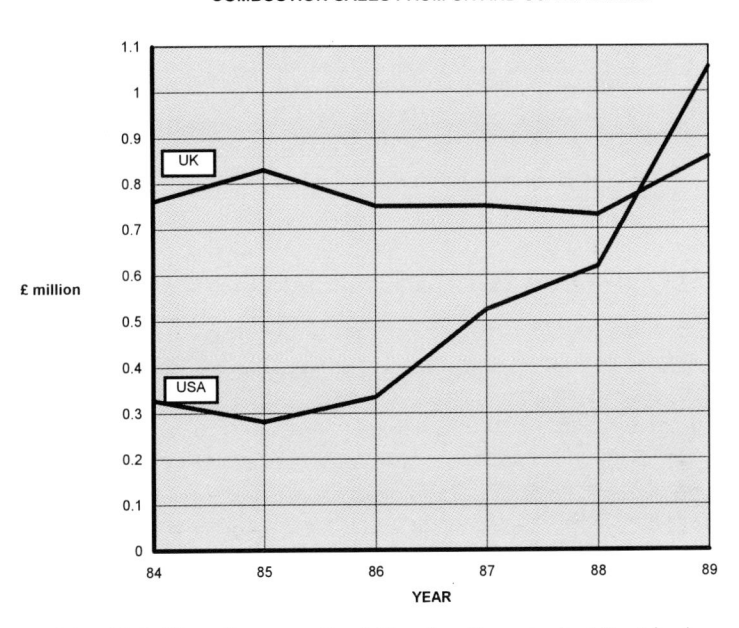

Fig. 11.2 How the growth of Combustion started first in America.

In addition to the support of THINK AMERICA from Dronfield Ramon had seen the opportunities for the resale of Oxygen Meters and Dust Monitors that his customers were already used to buying. He had decided to begin by importing good instruments of these kinds from Germany and from Japan. He would then proceed to develop better ones that we could make ourselves to replace the imports. This is the strategy followed for many decades by successful companies all over the world. Ramon also arranged for the German firm to sell our CO monitors in Germany, which was better still.

Happily there was more. Just at that time the market in combustion instruments in America was benefiting from a boom caused by new clean air legislation which gave a further impetus to the revival of our American business. With a better mix of more saleable products the European end of the business also began to revive. The combustion business began to have a clearer sense of direction and a powerful zip.

The driving force behind the growth in gas analysis equipment in America was the Environmental Protection Agency - the EPA. In the Western democracies, governments were increasingly realizing that they had a duty to protect our air, our rivers and our environment generally from the pollution that came from industrial processes and intensive farming. The first requirement of this policy was the installation of instruments to measure the pollutants, particularly noxious gases. The legal requirements laid down by the EPA produced a flood of business for manufacturers of gas analysis equipment. Living in the U.S.A., Ramon was close to this market and knew what it needed.

Ramon realized that the combustion instrument business had changed in character with the need to monitor noxious gases. In the past successful businesses had been able to concentrate on a single instrument such as a dust monitor or an oxygen analyser. Now many customers would need to buy a whole range of gas analysis instruments and the profitable opportunity had emerged for a company to market a complete range of instruments. The emergence of suppliers of reliable electrochemical cells made it possible for a business of our size to produce the range of instruments that the market needed. Ramon moved decisively to enter this market; he called the new approach 'the Total Efficiency Concept'. It comprised the following items:

Opacity and Dust Compliance Monitoring
Combustion Efficiency Monitoring
Environmental Emissions Monitoring
Portable Flue Gas Monitoring

This was a bold move. It makes sense to be able to provide this comprehensive range of instruments for the combustion engineer. To do so for the global market is going to need the most careful provision of support services. Opacity measurement was easily within the range of capabilities carried over from our optical design experience at Land Infrared. The oxygen analyser used for measuring combustion efficiency uses a well-established zirconia detector. The remaining instruments use the excellent range of electrochemical cells available commercially which form the basis of our portable gas analyser. The monitoring of 'environmental emissions' depends on the use of good commercially available equipment from America and Germany to solve the old problems of gas sampling.

We are fortunate to have a good level of expertise in electronic engineering which is critically important in all modern instrumentation. Like everyone today we wish that

LANDS RENEWED

we had more people skilled in the design of software and wish also that its cost were less daunting. At least we know how important it is going to be.

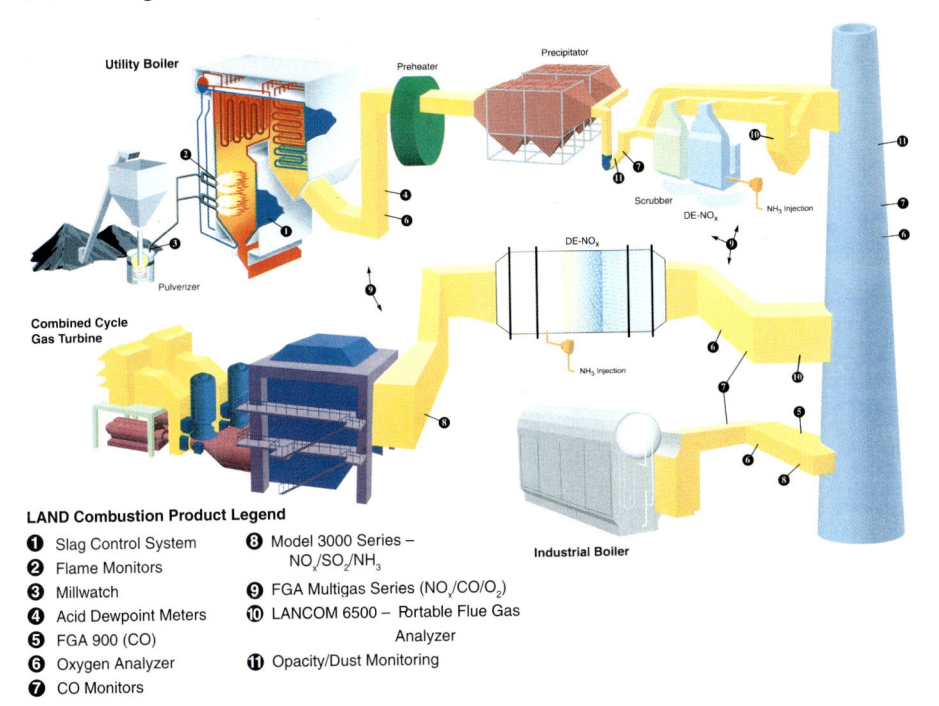

LAND Combustion Product Legend
1. Slag Control System
2. Flame Monitors
3. Millwatch
4. Acid Dewpoint Meters
5. FGA 900 (CO)
6. Oxygen Analyzer
7. CO Monitors
8. Model 3000 Series – $NO_x/SO_2/NH_3$
9. FGA Multigas Series ($NO_x/CO/O_2$)
10. LANCOM 6500 – Portable Flue Gas Analyzer
11. Opacity/Dust Monitoring

Fig. 11.3 Schematic diagram showing Land Combustion's application of products for 'The Total Efficiency Concept'.

One little detail is that the whole project would look much safer if we were about four times as big. But if we were, we would probably be sitting back with our feet on the desk while some little company crept up from nowhere and stole the show. Meanwhile we need to exercise discretion and concentrate on consolidating our present range of products, avoiding new ventures, however tempting, until we have nailed down the corners of the products that we have got. Now here are the specifications of our range of products that make up the 'total efficiency concept'.

Dust and opacity monitoring

We have designed the 4500 Mark II dust and opacity monitor with EPA compliance audits in mind. The built-in audit filter fixture makes quarterly auditing simple and quick to perform. An integral zero point reflector and span check filter are operated automatically to check the calibration of the instrument. The local control unit has a large LCD display. The accuracy meets and exceeds US EPA requirements 40 CFR 60.

Fig. 11.4 Model 4500 Opacity Monitor.

Combustion Efficiency

Combustion efficiency is usually monitored by measuring the oxygen content of the waste gas. Our Series 1200 oxygen meter is designed to fit into the flue at temperatures up to 600°C. It uses a zirconia sensor and displays the oxygen concentration on an LED with an accuracy of 1% of full scale.

Fig. 11.5 Series 1200 Oxygen Analyser.

Flue Gas Analysers

Our system for monitoring the emissions of carbon monoxide and the oxides of nitrogen depends on the use of advanced electrochemical cells. If a cell were used continuously for a long period its accuracy would drift off. We have therefore provided dual cells that are used alternately while the other is rested. This procedure ensures stable long term operation. The analysers also measure the oxygen concentration.

The FGA Series uses a sampling system. When we first began to design combustion instruments we were told that sampling systems caused endless trouble, so we set out to produce a range of gas analysers that would eliminate the need for sampling. But sampling has moved on and can be made much less troublesome. We now supply a range of heated and unheated probes, filters and hoses to suit the many different conditions encountered in industrial applications. There are heated filter probes, ceramic probes for hot conditions, water separating probes for wet gases as well as regulated and self-regulating heated sample lines.

The FGA 940 E and the FGA 950 E have fully automatic calibration systems, able to perform 2-point or 3-point calibrations without operator intervention. Every stage of the operation is controlled and monitored by the internal microprocessor.

Fig. 11.6 A typical FGA system.

The FGA 950E has been particularly successful in monitoring emissions from Combined Cycle Gas Turbine generating stations. We have designed a range of such systems to meet the needs of individual plants. Up on the stack or down on the ground, on walls, on frames, in cabins or in cabinets, with catalytic converters or without, and connected to every type of wiring standard, FGA 950 GTE systems are in their element on CCGT stations.

Portable gas analysers

Just as infrared thermometers are produced in fixed and portable systems, so there is a range of portable flue gas analysers to complement our fixed analysis installations. Our portable analysers rely on the same range of electrochemical sensors that are at the heart of the fixed FGA series.

In our inexperienced early days we wasted a lot of money trying to perfect an electrochemical cell that someone in Sheffield had invented. It was based on phosphoric acid and could be inserted into the hot gas stream without the use of the dreaded sampling systems. Unfortunately the inventor died soon after we took up his idea, which might explain why we were never really successful. It was always nearly successful, but in the end we had to abandon our efforts. The truth seems to be that in electrochemical detectors, just as in thermocouples or photoelectric arrays, it is not usually in the province of the instrument manufacturer to develop his own primary measuring elements. That is a job for a specialist who can do the job properly and supply the whole industry with a top quality product.

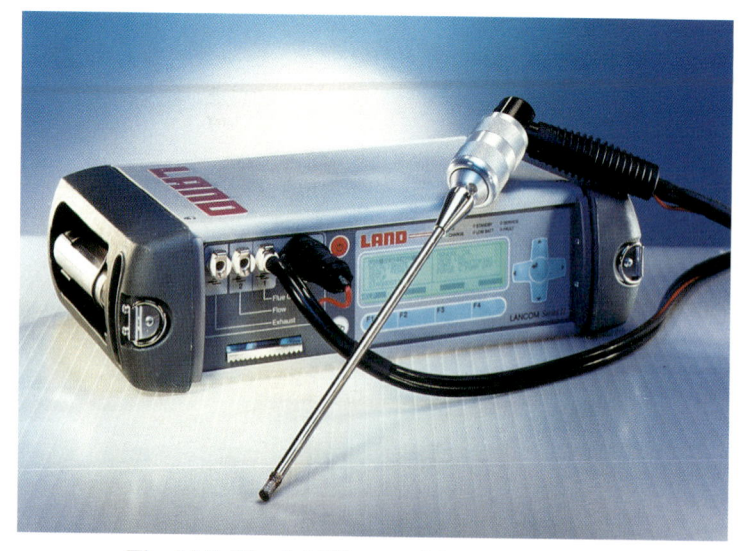

Fig. 11.7 The LAND portable gas analyser.

Our portable gas analysers are quite marvellous devices, capable of measuring as many as 7 different gases. The instrument weighs only 6kg (13lb) and is little bigger than a standard lap-top computer. It can be carried in the hand or slung on the shoulder. We have mounted the particulate and chemical filter cartridges on the side of the instrument where they are easy to see and the water catch-pot is mounted on a hinged assembly for easy removal and emptying.

All these products have been developed by Lands product development department under the direction of John Hyde. John and his fellow researchers have a substantial and well equipped laboratory where promising new instruments are developed and older ones are updated. Much of the technology is in electronics and physics, but software continues to grow in importance as our products have to interface with large computer systems.

Other products

In addition to these popular products we are able to offer updated versions of our earlier exotic instruments such as cross-duct CO monitors, Flamescan systems and acid dewpoint meters. Together these products form an impressive collection of high class products with more under development.

Production

Before writing this section I visited the works at Dronfield to see the latest facilities available for the assembly and testing of combustion instruments. Stuart King has most impressive facilities available as you will see from the illustration. Work stations are devoted to each class of instrument in a large airy room. Calibration and test facilities in the next room include the ability to test optical instruments over distances up to a surprising 60 metres.

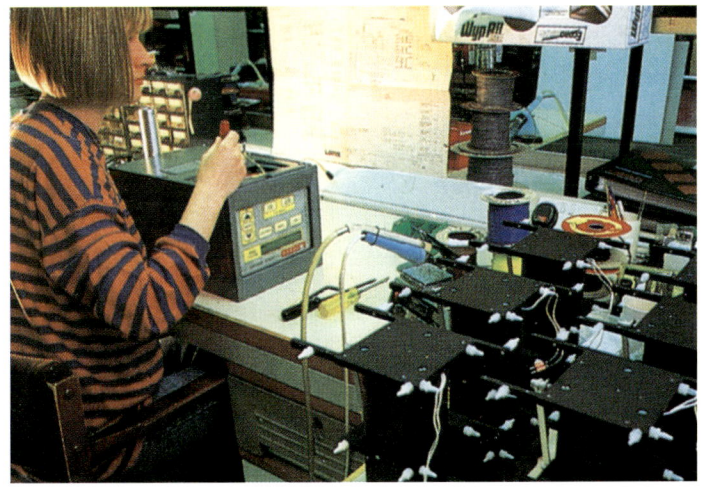

Fig. 11.8 The assembly room at Land Combustion.

As I looked at the new instruments that were coming through the Production Department, I realized that we were into a new world of chemical engineering. The gas analysers were boxes full of pipes and valves and solenoids and little electrochemical cells, not lenses and photoelectric cells and choppers. This was not physics, it was chemistry, as it should be. I felt less at home with it but strangely reassured that we had got it right.

Fig. 11.9 Ramon Biarnes and Dave Leadley receiving the ISO9001 certificate from NQA - recognising their commitment to quality products and services.

LAND INFRARED IN THE NINETIES

An accountant in charge of Land Infrared

The future of the Infrared Division after Roy Barber retired depended especially on the smooth co-operation of Tony Duncan and Geoff Beynon. Tony is a qualified accountant with a natural aptitude for business that had been put to the test and developed during the period that he was Managing Director of Land Pyrometers. But his scientific knowledge was not extensive. Geoff is an extremely thorough and competent scientist but his business experience at that time was not yet great. We just had to hope that the two of them would be able to work together. Thankfully they developed a mutual respect which has produced a stable basis for the management team running the Infrared Division which Roy had left behind. I am sure that Roy and Jasmine oversaw the transition with their usual care.

It was not easy to make good profits in the instrument industry during the early nineties because poor trading conditions discouraged our customers from ordering new equipment. Despite that, we decided to push ahead with a heavy investment programme.

It was decided as a first priority to establish our own subsidiary companies in Europe, first in Germany, then Italy and finally in France. Martin Johnston worked hard to ensure that all three were successful. Each is producing annual sales well above our expectations.

I have made a careful analysis of the financial implications of making the large investment needed to set up the three companies. As far as I can calculate the extra revenue generated has more than covered the start-up costs and left us with a far stronger company at the end. We have recently established Land KK in Osaka under our old friend Ike Sakaguchi. Now we are the truly international business that I believe to be essential for the future. We shall see if I am right.

One of the dangers of forming our own subsidiary companies was that our established distributors viewed this extension of our direct selling with some disquiet. The situation had to be handled with care. Tony and his sales team discussed it with them openly and with understanding. As a result the sales of Infrared products through distributors actually grew by nearly 100% in real terms during this decade.

In the U.S.A. Tony made a thorough study of the market potential and problems. He decided to increase the number of Area Managers and to locate them within their territories. Only one Area Manager operates from the head office at Bristol. The others were placed in Dallas (Texas), Pittsburgh, Circleville (Ohio), Chicago, Charlotte (North Carolina), and San Francisco. John Miller has now resigned and the new man would ideally be in Los Angeles. We must never forget how hard it is to take business from established market leaders. Tony's team are doing well and will deserve a special medal if they meet all their objectives.

Fig. 11.10 The Land Infrared sales and marketing team, and subsidiaries at the System 4 launch

Production

I have recently walked round the Production Department with David Chapman. Ten years ago I listened to Gary Plowman talking about the coming revolution in manufacturing that lay ahead with the full application of computers to engineering. Now I have seen the impact on our production department. I have also seen the effect of comprehensive and detailed co-operation of the Production Department with Product Development. This has been achieved throughout the design of System 4 and other new Infrared instruments. It certainly opened my eyes to a whole new world of engineering design and production where the needs of the customer and the possibilities of efficient production are given equal attention from the start of the project.

System 4

At the same time as we were opening up our wider sales organization and re-equipping our production facilities we decided to invest heavily in a new design of infrared thermometer. In this we abandoned, for the first time, the basic cylindrical shape of body, which would not accommodate the sighting system and the electronic circuitry which the market now requires. This elegant new system is now in production and looks to me to be a winner. Everyone tells me how much Ian Ridley contributed to the success of System 4, not least in the close liaison that he established with Production from the beginning of the design process.

Roy has told me how impressed he is by the quality of the optics and sighting systems. However, he reckons that the really clever bit was in making the original two processors compatible with all the thermometers. The original plan was that the system would be

Fig. 11.11 System 4 Thermometer and Processor.

LANDS RENEWED 163

limited to those two. Pressure, mainly from Germany, has resulted in further development of a stand-alone thermometer. This should also, for the first time, give us the means of attacking the OEM market. It will be very interesting to see how fast System 4 can take over from System 3. It is so much better and so much easier to make and calibrate.

Scanners

Our investment in new products has been by no means confined to System 4. At the same time we have continued to invest in several other special instruments that together produce more sales in some years than System 3 and System 4. One such special instrument is the Scanner. Most infrared thermometer applications require only a measurement at a single point on the hot surface, but on some occasions it is necessary to know how the temperature varies over a substantial area. If the hot surface is moving, as it is in a rolling mill, then we need only scan the temperature across the moving surface. A rotating mirror flashes the line of sight across the hot steel strip many times a second. We can then use a computer to build up a thermal map of the whole strip as it rolls under the scanner.

Fig. 11.12 Landscan in use.

Scanners had been around for a considerable time before we became involved. We were approached in the late 70's by Agema to see if we would like to develop and market their Linescan product. We decided not to take up their offer at the time, but we got into the market ourselves as a result of two events. Firstly, Ike Sakaguchi reported that the Japanese instrument company Chino were doing a lot of product development in this field. Secondly, we were approached by the Welsh Laboratories of the British Steel Corporation who were trying out some Agema equipment.

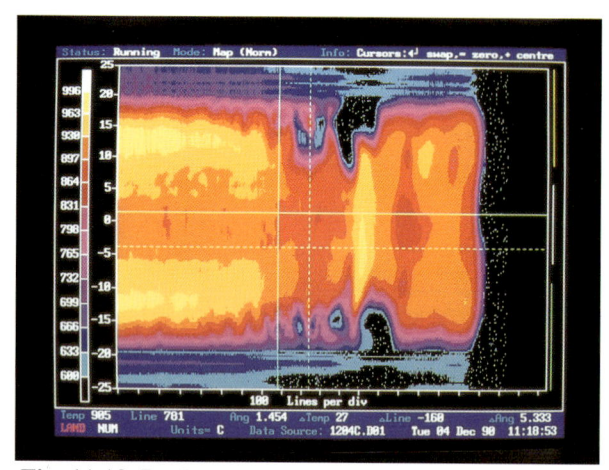

Fig. 11.13 Isotherms on a steel sheet during rolling.

Geoff went to see this, and felt that we could do better, both in accuracy and in robustness. He was proved to be right, and Welsh Labs. placed an order through a software systems house who supplied our heads with their software. We later realized that the real money lay in the system, and our software team put an immense amount of work into producing our own software. The scanners present a formidable data crunching problem, and the task continues. Meanwhile we have been steadily improving our design and finding new applications for this very successful product.

The first use of a scanner was to obtain a record of the temperature over the area of a hot-rolled steel strip. The customer buying the product could then be assured of the uniformity of its thermal history during the rolling process. To ensure uniformity of the product that his customer needs, the manufacturer may apply extra heating down the edges of the hot strip as it is being rolled. A scanner allows the heat to be applied in a controlled manner. To obtain the full benefits of a scanner its output must be passed to a computer. The software can be designed to give whatever form of temperature control the manufacturer chooses and whatever records the customer may demand.

Scanners have other uses. For example in a rolling mill making steel reinforcing bars the mill may be producing three strands simultaneously. It is impossible to stop the strands snaking across from side to side to a significant degree. A scanner can follow the three hot bars as they wander across the field of view. Suitable software will automatically follow them and make sure that each is rolled and quenched at a suitable temperature. The customer can also be given evidence of the thermal history of his product. Originally scanners could only operate at high temperatures using silicon cell detectors. Today we also manufacture scanners for lower temperatures down to 70°C, and for glass surfaces using radiation at a wavelength of 5 micrometres.

Thermal Imaging

When I returned to Dronfield from Sheepbridge in 1982 one of the first questions that Roy Barber asked me was whether I thought that we should spend a substantial amount of money to get into thermal imaging. It was not immediately obvious whether we should do so because thermal imaging was not then used much in industry. I thought about it carefully. Most industrial temperatures will always be measured at single points. They were then beginning to be measured (with scanners) along a line. They would inevitably begin to be required over an area. On this basis I said yes. I have no reason to think that we were wrong.

Although we are still only 'bit' players in this scene the market is going to be large and important to us. As in the case of scanners the secret of success is going to lie in the software. In this area we are already well placed. Thermal Imaging is being treated as a separate business, managed by John Dixon, for product development and assembly. The first wave of thermal imagers have been portable instruments using mirrors to scan the field of view. Our development of an excellent instrument of this kind was described in Chapter 9. It was always obvious that the commercial market would some day be able to follow military technology and develop the infrared equivalent of a video camera. This change is under way and we intend to be one of the participants. Meanwhile our excellent mirror system continues to sell well.

Fibre Optics

We first began to take fibre optics seriously when we found that it was essential to move the detector away from the sizzling heat in a jet engine. Once we had done that successfully it was natural to see that we could do the same in other places. So we began to make a range of special fibre optic installations in places such as spray chambers in the continuous casting of steel. In the glass industry it was natural to try fibre optics to take the detectors away from the heat of the feeders by the same technique. The general idea of using fibre optics is fairly obvious. The cleverness comes in the ability to provide fibre light guides that are robust enough to withstand the heat, the dirt and the intense vibration often present in an industrial installation.

Svet's idea in action

One day in the early nineties when I called in at Dronfield I learnt that a two-wavelength thermometer was successfully measuring the temperature of aluminium strip. Our patent, based on the equations that I had passed on to Geoff in the early eighties had at last been put into action and found to work. I was delighted. I had been aware that this was a long shot that just might do a useful job with a lot of care and a fair slice of luck. To find that it had been successfully applied to the most difficult industrial surface of all - aluminium - was wonderful.

The basic idea is that if you measure the apparent temperature of a surface at two different wavelengths it may be possible to identify which of a number of surfaces is being measured. In the case of aluminium alloys it is possible to distinguish between alloys containing different amounts of magnesium. We used an updated version of the Land surface pyrometer, with its gold-plated hemispherical reflector, as a reference standard to measure the true temperature of the aluminium alloy strip. A suitable circuit and a few days' experimental work allowed us to display the true temperature irrespective of the magnesium content of the alloy. It was a triumph of clever ideas and above all of extremely careful design and meticulous calibration. I was very proud that our technical team had achieved this outstanding break-through.

Product Philosophy

We have talked a great deal over the years about the 'product portfolio pyramid'. The peak is the very small volume of very expensive products. The broad base is the high volume "cheapies". Roy had moved us deliberately down from the peak, and there was pressure from some sources to go even further. Tony took a policy decision to try to halt, or even reverse the slide down. The best way to do this involved improving our systems capability, but in a controlled manner. In the past we have always acted as sub-contractors to systems companies. We are aware of the dangers involved in trying to supply total systems but it appears to be the way that the business must develop. I rather think that software is the key to the future.

Centralisation v. Localisation

One or two attempts were made to give more development and production responsibility to LII in America. For example they developed and made the Micratherm low temperature thermometer, and controlled the ground based turbine project. These were limited in success, and Tony has decided that, at least for the time being, he will centralise these functions at Dronfield. The success of this policy is demonstrated by the big step forward that was made when the ground based turbine project was taken over by Dave Amory when he returned to Dronfield. His return was a bonus, as he had done most of the on-site work in the U.S.A. and therefore knew the users' real needs. On the other hand Tony has increased the sales and marketing autonomy of the overseas companies, and he is happy with the results of this decision.

NEW BUILDING AT DRONFIELD

Our large investment during a serious recession went on for several years. I watched anxiously through those years as they stretched on and on. But the board continued to back the policy, believing that it would pay us handsome dividends in the end. Eventually the clouds broke, as they had done at the end of earlier recessions. I was reminded of the early nineteen sixties when our profits had suddenly soared after a recession, just in time to finance the building of the first stage of our Dronfield factory.

This time our return to good profitability enabled Jasmine to undertake some much needed extension and rebuilding that she had been planning for some time. She demolished much of the later additions to our factory that we had added during the seventies to house Land Pyrometers, which had now become ElectroNite UK and had gone elsewhere. Now we needed more factory space of a very different kind. Jasmine began with a new building joining our old factory to our more recently acquired extension on the Marples site next door.

Fig. 11.14 Aerial view of Land Instruments International Limited.

The new building has realigned the whole factory, placing the entrance where it should be, between the two factory blocks. It also turns the building literally back to front, so the it is now approached from Stubley Lane instead of from Wreakes Lane. This arrangement puts the main car parks sensibly behind the factory. The intention for the future is that Land Combustion should some day occupy the Marples building while Land Infrared should occupy new buildings to be built on the Land Pyrometers side. But, of course the future always has surprises waiting for us.

As we enter the new building through the reception area, we find that Jasmine's office has the Personnel office next to hers and the Information Technology headquarters opposite. This, to my mind, is exactly right for a modern business such as ours. People and the flow of knowledge are central to the whole operation. The new building also houses accommodation needed by both Divisions such as conference rooms, a dining room and some product development laboratory space. Our Dronfield factory now houses almost as many computers as people and our computing systems are constantly being updated and extended.

Fig. 11.15 The new entrance - 1997.

CHAPTER 12
QUALITY AND STANDARDS

A tradition of quality and accuracy

Most markets can be represented by a pyramid in which the height from the base is the quality of the products and the horizontal area at any particular height represents the numbers sold. In the British newspaper business we find the Times near the top of the pyramid and the Sun, with its big circulation, near the bottom. One difference between the two newspapers is that the Times is intensely proud of the accuracy of its news-stories while the Sun is proud of its circulation. In the instrument business Lands has always preferred to operate near the top of the pyramid and we, like the Times, are intensely proud of the quality and the accuracy of what we produce.

When I worked with my father in the electro-plate trade before the war he taught me to spend time walking round the factory examining the articles that were being made. I must make sure that handles were being put on exactly straight, that all file marks were being buffed out, that there were no scratches on the finished goods. It was always possible that an over-enthusiastic finisher might have polished off all the silver plate from a little patch of the surface. If there was any doubt I was taught to examine the reflection of the back of my hand in the polished silver which shows up the difference in colour between silver and the underlying metal. If the boss takes an interest in quality in this detailed way everyone becomes aware of its importance.

When I went on to Jessops the emphasis shifted to accuracy and standards. I needed standards of temperature against which I could check the instruments in use in the factory. I learnt to make a tubular furnace that had a long region of uniform temperature in the middle. I made up a standard platinum/platinum-rhodium thermocouple against which I could compare the output of the thermocouples that I brought in from the works. The two were bound together and put in my furnace and their outputs were compared. I realized that the reference standard would eventually be contaminated by the thermocouples from the works, so I kept a primary standard thermocouple against which I occasionally checked my working standard.

I had to check the accuracy of the optical pyrometers that we used to measure the temperatures of red-hot ingots and liquid streams. For this purpose I needed a standard of brightness. The General Electric Company made special lamps with filaments made of tungsten strip a couple of millimetres wide that could be lit up using a car battery. We had each lamp calibrated at the National Physical Laboratory at Teddington. They returned it to us with a certificate stating the current required to produce a brightness corresponding to each specified temperature when using a disappearing filament optical pyrometer. The NPL pyrometer would have been calibrated on a black-body furnace of known accuracy in relation to the International Temperature Scale. This chain of comparison back to the International Temperature Scale is now known as 'traceability' and is central to all calibration procedures.

My work with Donald Oliver on the Liquid Steel Sub-Committee brought me in touch with physicists at the National Physical Laboratory. I was determined that everything that I did at Jessops would to be at a level of accuracy that would be fully acceptable at the NPL. I carried this approach with me when I set up Land Pyrometers after the war. Roy Barber started his working life with Mr Todd and his assistant David Cresswell in the Research Department at Hadfields in Sheffield where equally rigorous standards prevailed.

Land Infrared

I found at quite an early stage in my work at Queens Road that there were many steelworks laboratories that had a need for the same sort of equipment that I had developed at Jessops for calibrating optical pyrometers. We therefore designed a unit that comprised a strip-filament lamp, with its Giant Edison Screw lamp-holder, together with a specially designed clamp that would hold all the models of pyrometer in use at that time. The pyrometer could be accurately adjusted to sight on the correct spot on the filament and a magnifying lens of special clear glass. The unit also had knobs for coarse and fine adjustment of the direct current obtained from a battery and an accurate 4-terminal resistor of one thousandth of an ohm to provide a means of measuring the lamp current with a laboratory potentiometer. The unit is illustrated in Fig. 12.1.

Fig. 12.1 Our first optical pyrometer calibrating unit.

QUALITY AND STANDARDS

When we began to make infrared thermometers in the 1950s we did not only have to design a new breed of accurate thermometers. We also had to design a new breed of accurate calibration equipment. We already had the strip lamp for the highest temperatures but it was not suitable for the 'total radiation' pyrometers that we first made. We needed a good black body furnace with a large sighting aperture. We were fortunate that BISRA had invented the spherical black body furnace for high temperatures. For lower temperatures we had to devise a black body source whose uniform temperature was guaranteed by immersing it in a stirred liquid. To calibrate the Land Surface Pyrometer we had to design a steel hot plate of known and uniform surface temperature. Roy and I spent a great deal of time calculating the radiative properties of spheres and tubes and checking our results in the laboratory.

Fig. 12.2 The calibration laboratory at Dronfield in 1969 with Dick Nicholson taking measurements.

Visitors to the company were not only impressed with the quality of our products, they were also impressed with the quantity and quality of our calibration equipment. When we moved to Dronfield we had a large room upstairs which housed both the product development laboratory and the calibration area which is illustrated in Fig. 12.2. Customers who had purchased a significant number of radiation thermometers were interested in establishing their own calibration facilities. As requests to purchase our sources increased we decided that they should became Land products in their own right. The Land spherical furnace became the world's first commercially available temperature source for the calibration of radiation thermometers. Many are still in use today. Demands for wider temperature span and greater accuracy over the years resulted in a calibration equipment portfolio which now contains a choice of 8 different designs of source covering the temperature range -10°C to 1600°C.

Around 1960 I was still under the delusion that we would become a 'real instrument company', manufacturing indicators, recorders and controllers like others in the industry. In preparation for this glorious future I decided that we could set up a service department servicing other people's instruments in our region of the country. This was a profit centre that would also give us a detailed insight into the strengths and weaknesses of existing products. Peter Henderson was in charge of this Service Department. This section eventually came under the wing of the calibration department.

When we began to make Dipstiks under licence from ElectroNite we initially had trouble in getting reliable measurements and this led us to invite David Cresswell to join our little team, which he did. We had bought a small induction furnace in which we could melt a small amount of steel to test our Dipstiks. We developed a method of checking a Dipstik in liquid steel at the melting point of palladium, which is within the usual range of steelmaking temperatures. We did so by the well-established method of including a short length of palladium wire at the hot junction of the thermocouple. As the liquid steel was slowly heated above 1550°C the palladium wire melted as it reached its melting point and this was clearly seen on the temperature record. We were surprised at the accuracy of this calibration, which we used on a routine basis for many years.

In addition to this work and such interesting projects as the parrot's perch experiment, David Cresswell took over the maintenance of our calibration standards. Customers began to ask us to check their equipment for them and in 1968 Mike E. Brown was engaged as an assistant to David Cresswell to extend this part of our business.

I must break into the story here to point out that we now had two different people called Mike Brown in important positions in the company. This one fortunately is called Mike E. Brown and although his namesake is no longer with us he is still usually called by that name. In this book I think it is always pretty obvious which one I am writing about. Mike E. Brown never went to live and work in America.

We could now offer a very accurate calibration service which many customers preferred to the more expensive alternative of sending their equipment to the National Physical Laboratory. We reported our calibration figures in a Land certificate.

Obviously the British Government must have been watching what we were doing with their usual close attention. Within a year or two they announced the establishment of the British Calibration Service (BCS). The main reason for the establishment of the

QUALITY AND STANDARDS

BCS was to relieve the NPL of routine certification work to allow them more time to concentrate on the maintenance and development of national standards. The plan was to utilize existing commercial laboratory facilities to offer a nationally and internationally recognisable calibration service. Roy immediately saw the advantages of this proposal and gave it his full support.

Any laboratory could apply to join this service, but before they were accepted a team of experts from the NPL visited the laboratory to asses its capabilities. They interviewed the people, inspected the equipment and the laboratory environment, examined the procedures and records and assessed the handling and despatch procedures. In 1970 we became the first thermal measurements laboratory to be accepted, with Roy Barber as Head of Laboratory. We could then issue to our customers British Calibration Certificates acceptable world-wide. Roy handed over to David Cresswell in 1974, who was followed in 1976 by Mike Brown who still holds the position. In 1985 BCS became NAMAS. We are the only laboratory in Britain able to offer on-site certification of radiation thermometers. Every year we issue more certificates than the year before and in 1996/7 we issued more than 850.

Fig. 12.3 Some of our modern calibration equipment.

Quality control has been around for a long time in the best businesses. In recent years there has been a decisive shift by large companies who now insist that their suppliers should meet international documented quality standards. Our quality system has been assessed by Lloyds Register Quality Assurance and found to meet requirements for BS EN ISO9001 : 1994 for the design, manufacture, repair and on-site servicing of non-contact temperature measuring equipment; also for BS EN ISO9002 for stockholding of Minolta/Land portables and the relative Civil Aviation Authority requirements. All this quality control work is done by Mike's department.

The sales of calibration equipment make only a modest contribution to our Infrared sales, but the department, which is responsible for the accuracy and the quality of all the equipment that is sold, is of crucial importance to the whole enterprise. Mike and his staff are rightly proud of the contribution that they make to the reputation of the Company as an enterprise of quality and distinction.

Land Combustion

Land Infrared deals only with the calibration of one kind of instrument, infrared thermometers, and serves a wide diversity of markets. Infrared thermometers have been around in one form or another for a long time. Indeed the International Temperature Scale is defined over a wide range of temperatures by measurements using a radiation thermometer. Land Combustion is different. It serves a narrowly defined market, but into this market it sells a wide variety of instruments, all of which need to have their calibrations traceable to internationally acceptable institutions.

Fortunately the gas analysis instruments can all be calibrated in the same way. It is possible to buy cylinders of gases of known composition, usually mixtures of a single gas with a much larger proportion of nitrogen. The suppliers guarantee the composition of the gas mixtures to be accurately traceable to a national standards laboratory. The standard gas is passed through the gas analyser whose output is adjusted to match the stated composition of the gas in the cylinder. The instrument can be designed to perform such an operation automatically at prescribed intervals on site.

The acid dewpoint meter measures the temperature at which sulphuric acid begins to be deposited on a glass surface, exposed to the furnace gases, when the opposite surface of the glass is cooled by a stream of cool air. The temperature of the outer surface is measured by a platinum rhodium thermocouple whose accuracy of calibration is traceable through its manufacturers to the National Physical Laboratory.

The dust monitor is calibrated by reference to a set of neutral density glass plates whose transmission is traceable through their manufacturers to the NPL or the NIST in the USA. In America the Environmental Protection Agency is satisfied with measurements of the opacity of the products of combustion. In Europe it is sometimes necessary to provide means to convert the opacity into milligrams of dust per cubic metre of gas and this has to be done on site for a particular plant or process.

CHAPTER 13
SOME THINGS THAT I HAVE LEARNT

What we have achieved together in 50 years

When I drive past our factory in Dronfield or walk through the workshops, offices and laboratories, I feel very proud of what we have achieved in the past 50 years. We have created it all, not quite from nothing, but from relatively little. We have built a fine business and in doing so we have learnt a great deal about how a business should be run. In this final chapter I am setting down some of the things that I have learnt myself and some of my personal views on business and management.

When I walk round the factory and talk to the people who work there I soon notice that I am not the only person to feel intense pride in being part of a fine business. This is good for the business, and it is also good for the people who work in it. We need to feel proud of ourselves as individuals and as members of a fine community. We may be proud of our family, of the teams that we support, of the achievements of our country. Such pride enhances our lives and, I am sure, improves our health and enjoyment of being alive.

From an early stage in the growth of our new business I realized that I was not one of those wonderful people who seem to have unlimited energy. The business has had to be the creation of many people. I knew that there were certain things that I was very good at but that there were many more that other people were capable of doing as well and better. So I made it a rule that I would try not to do the things that others could do equally well; I would concentrate my rather limited energy on the things that I could not comfortably delegate to other capable people.

This turned out to be a strength, not a weakness. It gave me more time to do the things that a manager should do. I believe that the most important part of a manager's job is to help the people who work for him to be better at their jobs. For example when we began to develop closer ties with ElectroNite during the middle eighties I saw the chance to learn from Henk Kleyn by watching how he handled opportunities and difficulties in his business. But the person who could benefit most from that experience at that time would be not myself but Tony Duncan who was new to the job of Managing Director of Land Pyrometers. So I took every opportunity to encourage an increasingly close relationship between Henk and Tony, not me, so that Tony could become a better Managing Director. In such ways, over the years, I worked to develop the talents of the many people who built the business with me.

A working community that makes money and serves its customers well

Over the last fifty years we have created two things of quite different kinds. We have built a working community of people developing, manufacturing and selling instruments. We have also made sufficient money over the years to build the factory at Dronfield and a smaller one outside Philadelphia, to buy all the machines and equipment, the stock on the shelves and much more. Business, you see, is about people working together and it is at the same time about the accumulation of money. Unless money is accumulated and put to use nothing can be achieved.

But our most important achievement of all is something that you cannot see as you walk through the factory. It is the respect and loyalty that we have earned from hundreds of customers all over the world who have bought our instruments and have found them accurate, reliable and well suited to their needs. That is what our business exists to do, to serve our customers better than our competitors do, to be aware of our customers' changing needs and to provide them with the best advice and equipment at competitive prices.

A business cannot afford to stand still. The rapid development of technology is constantly expanding both our customers' need for instrumentation and our ability to create new and better equipment. We must drive ahead or be left stranded, and progress costs loads of money. The business must be profitable enough to provide (at the time of writing) nearly £2 million a year for product development and as much again to provide enough, after paying dividends and taxes, to finance our growth.

Concentration and world-wide sales

I have learnt that to be successful we must concentrate our efforts in a few narrowly defined markets and products and we must sell those products in all the major countries of the world. If we made too wide a range of products we would spread our effort too thinly. We would then be unable to match the expenditure on product development of our competitors and we would be overwhelmed and left behind. American manufacturers may be able to rely solely on obtaining a dominant position in their big, wonderful home market, but a British company must sell world-wide. Only in this way can we generate enough money to support an adequate programme of product development and also invest enough in the growth of the business.

The best businesses find at least one major product line in which they are so far in advance of the competition that they dominate the market. Many of the best German middle-sized companies have achieved just this. We have one or two opportunities to do so and we should make very great efforts to ensure that we really do achieve it in our business. Land Pyrometers held this enviable position in the U.K. market for many years thanks to the ElectroNite patents; patents can be a critical component in success of this kind.

Good people at the heart of the business

Success in our business depends on recruiting and training very good people and engaging their enthusiasm. In any creative business one first class person can achieve more than two less talented and unmotivated employees. So it is most important to attract good people to work for us and to give them interesting and challenging projects. If we want them to stay with us we must pay them enough to make them glad to stay.

People work enthusiastically when they are given clearly defined tasks that are within their capacity to achieve and when they understand the part that they play in a well-conceived overall programme. So we must have good managers. Above all we need first-class people at the heart of the business. Everyone must be keen but these few people must be keen as mustard. We have had to learn that if someone in such a position is not up to his job we must harden our hearts and replace him (or her) without delay. When you have to do that you have made a big mistake yourself and promoted someone beyond his ability and, by definition, lost yourself a very good man. We all do it, no matter how hard we try to make good judgements and, when we do, we feel bitterly disappointed and ashamed of our poor judgement.

These few people have the job of steering the company in the right direction. They need to understand our business and have the vision to see what it could and should become. They need to have the courage to spend money when it should be spent and the prudence to say no to projects that we cannot and should not afford. They must have the humility to ask for help and to seek out opinions from others whose judgement they respect, but in the end they must make a decision themselves, knowing that a few of their decisions will be quite wrong and some more will prove to be not all that clever. Above all they must have the courage to make a clear decision for others to follow and take the rap when occasionally they are wrong.

The people who direct the business must not allow themselves to be isolated in their offices looking at reports, attending meetings and thinking profound thoughts. They must get out and about the business, talking to the people who are making things and who are selling our goods at home and abroad. They must know exactly what new things are being cooked up in the Product Development Department and how the projects are progressing. They must have the humility and good sense to ask everyone what they think about the things that we are doing and take a lot of notice of what they say. The people closest to the action know most.

The organization

It is usual to represent the organization of a business in the same way as a family tree with the Managing Director sitting at the top and the successive layers of managers fanning out below him. I think that it is more helpful to imagine the Managing Director as being at the centre of the business. The people in charge of the various functions such as manufacturing and selling are each at the centre of their own group of people.

The family tree suggests that the only thing that flows through the system is authority. There is far more to it than that and in any case the flow must never be all in one direction.

I would suggest that there are three main things that flow through the business. Of course the thing that flows fastest is rumour. The business is suddenly thought to be in deep trouble and the whole Product Development Department is going to be shut down! Rumours are a form of panic and spread with the speed of a forest fire in a hot dry summer. If only we could make useful things flow where they are needed as easily! Three useful and important things that flow through the business come to my mind.

Direction. If a business is to be successful everybody in the organization must know very clearly the objectives that are being pursued and what his own part in the plan should be. Authority and clear guidance on the implementation of the objectives must flow freely everywhere. This can lead to the common mistake of believing that everything should be planned from the top, and it is not only communists that make that mistake. It is the job of the few people at the centre to plan the broad strategy of the business. Everyone has a part to play in implementing the detail and it is the person nearest the action who often knows best what needs doing. Peter Drucker has written wisely on this subject. In a well-run organization each manager will, at regular intervals, ask each person responsible to him to tell him what are the things that he thinks he can undertake to deliver in the coming period. He is likely to know what is needed in greater detail than his boss, but the manager must be ready, if necessary, to say 'no, that is not what we need you to do'. This procedure makes each person think carefully for himself what the company needs from him - or, of course, from her.

Money. It says in the Nursery Rhyme that 'the King was in his counting house, counting out his money'. Today the small shopkeeper still counts out his money and takes it to the Bank in a bag at the end of the day. In a business like ours money is hardly ever seen, but it is there all right and it flows everywhere. The accounting system is designed to track it down and the Management must make sure that it flows into the right places. Above all more must flow into the business than flows out, otherwise calamity arrives fast.

Knowledge. The flow of knowledge in a business is absolutely vital to its successful operation. It is amazing that it is not studied more systematically. Everyone who works at Lands has experience of our Information Meetings. When the business was much smaller I used my speech at the Christmas luncheon party to tell everyone how things were going and to announce new plans and new benefits. As the business grew bigger we decided that we needed to institute a more formal procedure. But knowledge is flowing everywhere. Think how we convey information about our products to our customers through personal visits, through sales literature left with the customer, through advertising, mail shots, video displays, exhibitions and presentations. But this is only one side of a two-way process. It is equally important that knowledge should flow freely from the customer to us. We need to understand the many processes in our customers' plants where our equipment might be useful, to understand them well enough to suggest applications that they might not have thought of themselves. We also need to have a good flow of knowledge about how well our instruments are performing in service so that we can rectify any defects and promote applications that have proved successful. Within our business knowledge about new products must flow rapidly from Product Development engineers to the Production Department and to the Sales and Publicity people. Then there is all the knowledge that is stored in people's brains which leads us into the whole subject of training. There is knowledge stored in books, which takes us into the library. A great deal of useful knowledge is now stored in computers as text and as drawings which can be transmitted and printed out throughout the organization and this will become of increasing importance in the future.

When I read Roy Barber's contribution to Chapter 9 I came to the section in which he described how he engaged consultants to teach him about marketing. In commenting on the many meanings ascribed to the word 'marketing' he concluded that it was essentially KNOWLEDGE. The capital letters were his, not mine. I think that he is right. Of course there is more - insight, imagination, lateral thinking. But the study of the flow of knowledge in a business is central to the understanding of the business.

Removing the barriers to enthusiasm

People go out to work primarily to earn a living. Sometimes they never move beyond that minimum commitment. If we want them to do more and to be enthusiastic about their jobs we have to ensure that they become committed members of a working community. We have learnt over the years some of the things that must be done to achieve this.

People love to be part of a successful enterprise. It must have been wonderful to play football for Liverpool or Manchester United in recent years. Tens of thousands of fans go to Anfield or Trafford Park just to watch them play and become a singing, cheering part of that success. In running a business it is all too easy to erect barriers that inhibit the natural development of enthusiasm and commitment. Good managers identify those barriers and set about removing them.

First of all we have to remember that there would not be much enthusiasm at Anfield if the fans could not see what was happening on the pitch. As our business has grown we have learnt that we must organize small meetings to tell everybody what is happening in the business. We find that we can safely tell them the truth about everything - how the orders are coming in, how much profit is being made, how it is being invested in the business, why things are being done, what we hope to achieve.

This openness is linked to the fact that everyone gets a share of the profits that the business makes. Of course there is a pressing need for a sufficient proportion of the profit to be retained in the business to finance our growth and for shareholders to receive an appropriate dividend on their investments. When everyone gets a share of the profits then everyone wants to see big profits and an efficiently run company. Each employee of Lands receives a share of the profit proportional to their remuneration. It makes a big difference to the way that people feel about their company when each gets 'a share of the action'.

We firmly believe that our business should have no second class citizens. Everyone at Dronfield has 'staff status' and is paid a monthly salary by bank transfer. Everyone in the U.K. belongs to the same pension plan and the same private health insurance plan and has the same same sickness benefits. Of course pay is determined by the level of remuneration for similar jobs elsewhere in the same country and holiday entitlements are graded according to responsibility and length of service. Employees in different countries must have all these different rewards adjusted to common practice in each area, and we try to make them fair and acceptable. It is not easy but we try our best and don't do too badly. The vital principle is that there should be no distinction between 'staff' and 'workpeople'. This would be distinction by class and has no place at all in a business community.

In such ways we aim to remove the psychological barriers that all too easily grow between 'them' and 'us'. When we are all treated alike, when we all know what is happening in the business and why, and when all share financially in the success of our enterprise there is a very different feeling in the organization. We can then all develop a natural pride in being part of a winning team, a belief that we can be the best and a dedication to the success of the enterprise.

Learning the skills

These factors affect our state of mind in approaching our tasks but they do not, in themselves, get the jobs done well. Our early efforts at being engineers were pitiful and we needed to employ someone who knew how to do things in a professional way. At least we did not have ingrained bad working habits that had to be unlearnt. Throughout our 50 years in the instrument business we have been learning new skills from inventory control to marketing and software writing. Continuous improvement, the continuous acquisition of new skills, and continuous cost reduction are basic requirements of any business.

Financial control

We have had to be careful as we have grown to keep our financial systems improving. We are fortunate that Jasmine is not only an experienced manager with qualities of leadership, but also a very competent qualified accountant capable of handling the complexities of a business working in many currencies across the world. She has ensured that we have a modern computer system that covers adequately not only the accounting needs of our international business but also the scientific and technical requirements of a business such as ours.

Companies of our size and complexity would commonly have a Financial Controller among its top management staff. Jasmine combines that position with that of Group Managing Director with great efficiency. When inflation ran into double figures in the seventies and Tony Duncan was our accountant, he and I devised a good system which eliminated from our management accounts the large errors that would otherwise be caused by inflation. Jasmine has polished and refined that system which we still keep running in case inflation should become a serious problem again.

A good place to work

The most obvious lesson is perhaps the most significant. I have always believed that a sense of community in the business is important above all to the individuals who work at Lands. We spend a great part of our lives at our place of work and it matters very much indeed to our happiness that we should work in a community in which we are at ease, welcome and cared for. A family business need not be a heartless institution. But it must at all costs be economically efficient because that is its function and for that reason it may occasionally be necessary to make staff reductions. It must make plenty of money or it will be destroyed by its competitors. But in a family business the management can afford to have care, consideration and compassion for the people that work as part of the community. When it does so it creates a cohesive, efficient unit and a good place to spend our working days.

The future

For a million years and more our ancestors lived and worked in groups of a few hundred people all of whom knew each other. It is hardly surprising that many studies have shown this to be the most efficient and congenial size of unit for all sorts of activity, including business. We have a business of that size at Dronfield. But to function efficiently in the modern world that friendly, efficient Dronfield unit must extend internationally all round the globe. How do we make all the people who work for us in America, Italy, Japan, Germany, France and elsewhere feel themselves to be part of that same community? And every bit as important, how do we stop the people at Dronfield feeling that all these people overseas are alien to their group? In the past our business has grown about ten times bigger every twenty-five years. That may seem like a heck of a time when you are twenty, but believe me when you are eighty you know it goes in no time. If we go on as we have done in the past you are going to have lots of interesting problems to solve. You, not me!

It has struck me forcibly as I have been writing that the future has always turned out to be much more wonderful than anything that I had ever imagined that it could be. In calling the book 'LANDS so far' I have intended to emphasise how true that still remains. The future of Lands will always amaze you.